THIS FILM
SHOULD BE PLAYED
LOUD

Playlist No. 0

-Jazz Suite No. 2: VI. Waltz II/Shostakovich

-The Tattooed Bride/Duke Ellington

-Where Flamingos Fly/Gil Evans

-Riot/Miles Davis

-Dakar/John Coltrane

-Gunslinging Bird/Charles Mingus

-Videotape/Christian Scott aTunde Adjuah

-Truth/Kamasi Washington

-Moment of Hesitation/Flying Lotus

-Glass Bead Games/Jeremy Pelt

- Aske Me Now/Melissa Aldana

-54 Cymru Beats/Donny McCaslin

Crate Digging

B-sides, Rarities & Outtakes

From

This Cinematic Life

by Craig Duffy

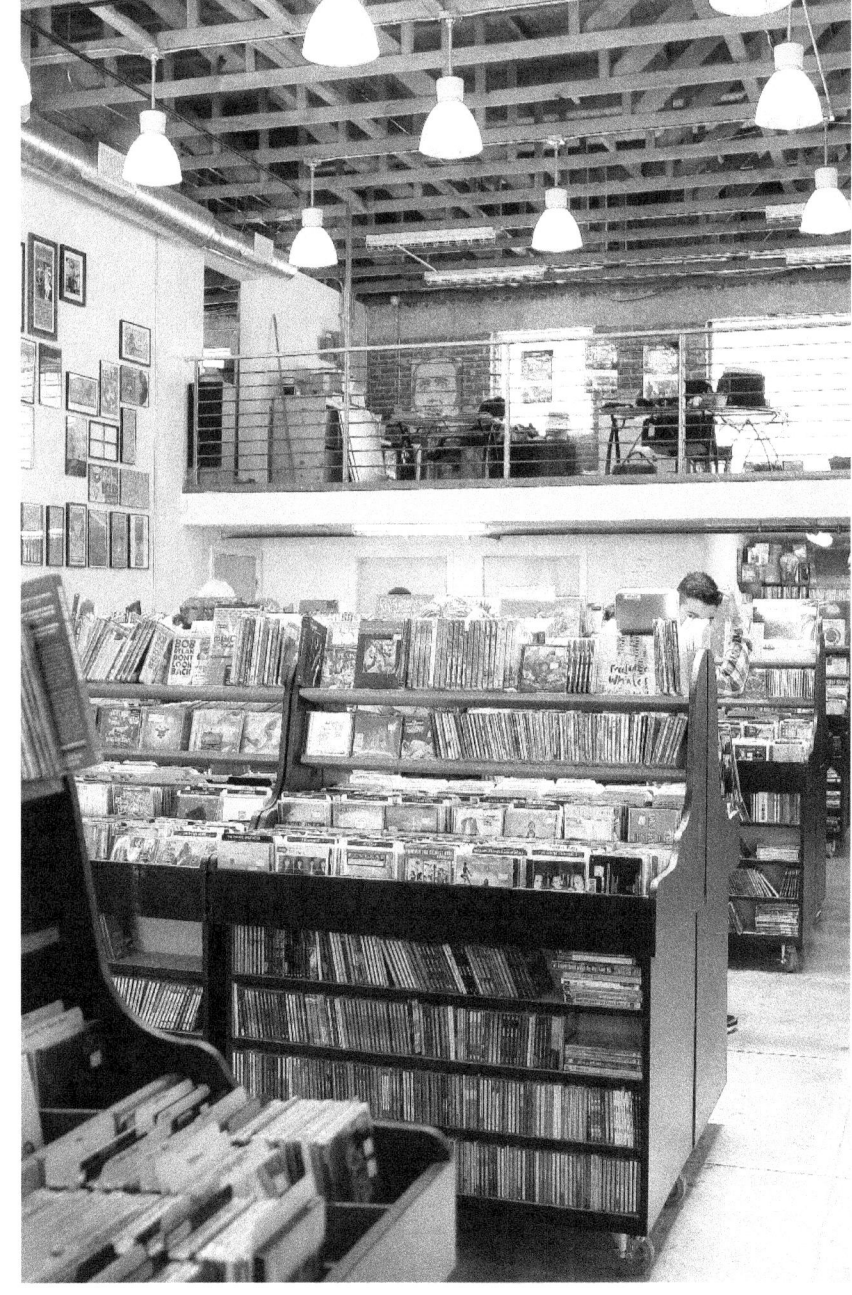

For Mark Harris and J. Hoberman

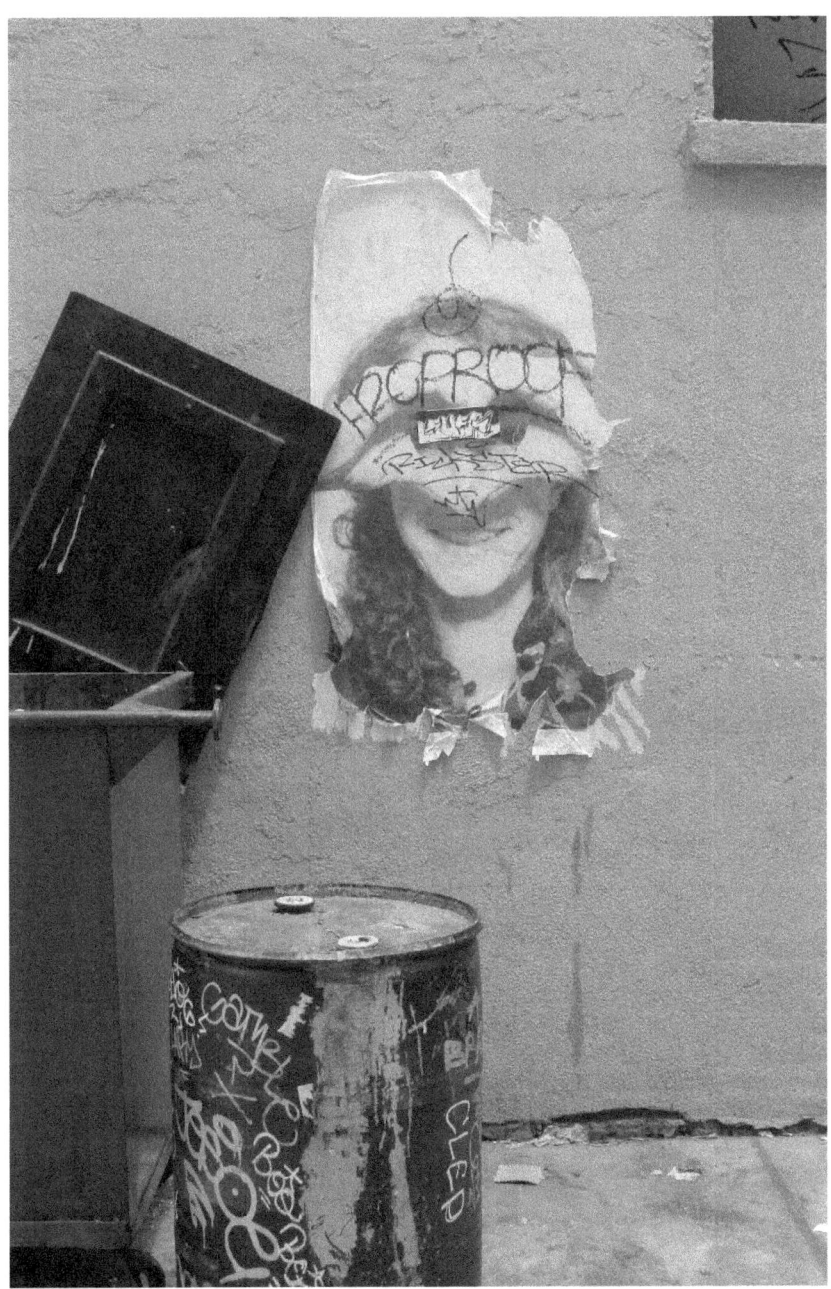

Table of Contents

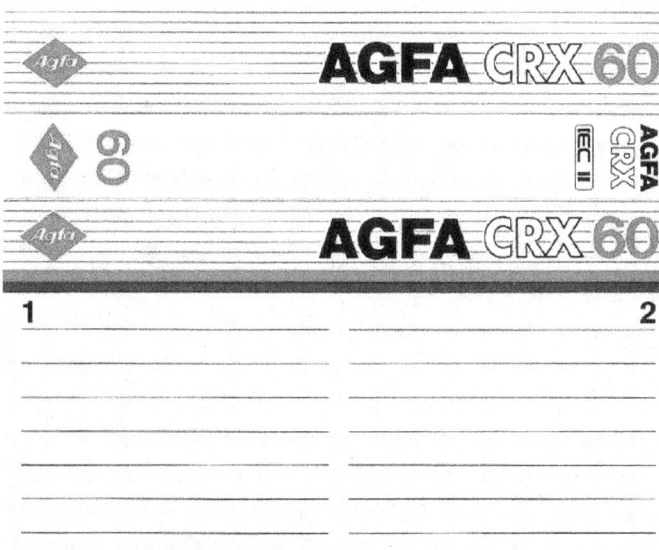

AGFA CRX 60

Agfa

60 *Agfa* IEC II AGFA CRX

AGFA CRX 60 *Agfa*

1   2

maxell UR
POSITION
IEC TYPE I • NORMAL

UR   maxell

Ⓐ DATE _____ . _____ . Ⓑ DATE _____ . _____ .
N.R.   ○ YES ○ NO   N.R.   ○ YES ○ NO

Intro

The first David Lynch film I ever saw was *Lost Highway*. I'd like to say that this was because in Middle School I was already a very discerning, young cinephile. But the truth is that my friends and I had found a video store that would rent us R-rated movies and we had heard that there was nudity in this one. Like Jeffrey Beaumont in *Blue Velvet*, I was looking for titillation. What I found was something else entirely. I discovered a world of darkened corners capable of containing entire universes, where the soundtrack rumbles and images flicker in and out of focus. It's a world Special Agent Dale Cooper might describe as, "both wonderful and strange." This was the start of an obsession that still consumes me two decades later.

While I hold several directors in extremely high regard, it's the work of David Lynch that I find myself pondering most often. A large portion of this can be attributed to the amount of ambiguity he employs in his work. His films are like a song lyric you cannot quite complete, so you cycle it endlessly in your brain. The cinematic equivalent of an Ear Worm. But to limit his Cinema to this one aspect is about as profound as that, "You've been Lynched" meme. In David's world, the things missing and left unsaid are more than willful obfuscation.

For me, the closest analogue for the Cinema of David Lynch, is Opera. It's a world of emotion so heightened that even if you don't speak the language of the libretto, you innately understand what is being expressed. Like how everyone in the town of Twin Peaks knows that Laura Palmer is dead without even having to be told. The air is so thick with sorrow that you cannot help but know.

This is enhanced by the recurrent motif of performance that can be found throughout Lynch's Work. From the Woman in the Radiator of *Eraserhead*, to Dorothy Vallens at Slow Club in *Blue Velvet*, to Julee Cruise in The Road House of *Twin Peaks*, to Rebekah Del Rio in *Mulholland Dr.*'s Club Silencio, important revelations are constantly being transmitted through music. And it's not as simple as a character hearing a song that the early part of the film has taught us to find important. It's not a matter of lyrics either. It's performers being used as vessels for messages from beyond. Within the context of the narrative, that performer is often communicating something from another dimension. Within the context of us watching a film, they are communicating something from the soul of David Lynch.

And like the silent filmmakers of old, Lynch also employs as little dialogue as possible. Of course people do talk in his films, but as critic Dennis Lim describes in his book <u>The Man from Another Place</u>, "Lynch's films abound with gnomic pronouncements and incantations." Lim also compares phrases like "Now it's dark" and "This is the girl" to meditative mantras used in Lynch's beloved Transcendental Meditation. The words are not there to give exposition, they're there to cast a spell. In his recent biography <u>Room to Dream</u>, numerous Lynch actors tell stories of David being able to illicit a performance with a single word, or even a hand gesture. This jives well with Lim's observation that, "Lynch seems less to be stonewalling than striving to verbalize daunting concepts with a vocabulary that might politely be termed basic." And I think that's why I relate so strongly to his work.

I too am attempting to communicate the ineffable. And not just in the sense that I am using the written word to talk about a visual and aural medium. Yes, that's a part of it. But on a deeper level, it's the fact that I'm using the art of others to express myself. I'm like that new boyfriend who makes you a mixtape to say all the things he doesn't have words for. Even when I'm writing about how a certain film reflects the state of the world or the lives of the people who made it, I'm still talking about myself. I'm never going to write an autobiography, but I'd like to think that if you've read my criticism, you know me.

This book is my mixtape. I made it just for you.

*   *   *

As with my previous book, I've organized the capsule reviews around theme as follows…

-How movies relate to their authors

-How movies relate to other movies

-How movies relate to the world

-How movies relate to me personally

Unlike the previous book, I have included new material that never appeared on the blog. Some of these pieces were intended to become blog posts but never made it further than my personal Letterboxd account (username: cduffy) and there is also the long-read piece about the 80th Academy Awards that is the completed version of a piece I started on the blog back in 2012.

I'm not sure if I will ever return to regular blogging so I'm really throwing in everything I can. I hope you are able to get something out of it. I really got something out of writing it.

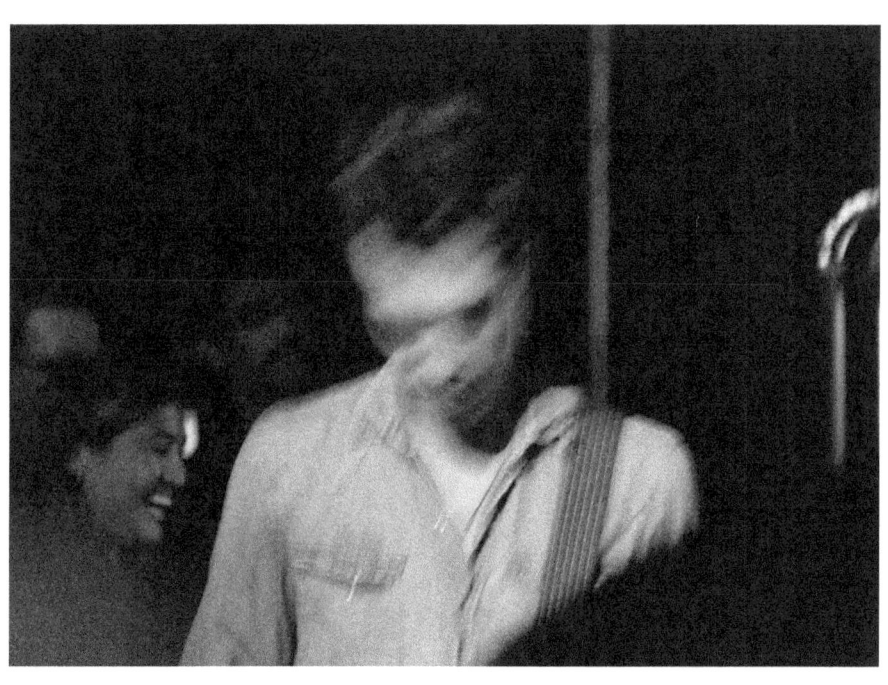

Playlist No. 2

-Third Stone from the Sun/The Jimi Hendrix Experience

-Redondo Beach/Patti Smith

-Wave of Mutilation/Pixies

-Mini Skirt/Performers

-Them Changes/Thundercat

-No Big Bang/Priests

-Lady Day & John Coltrane/Gil Scott-Heron

-La course de Manuel (Chase)/Mikis Theodorakis

-Theme from the Persuaders/John Barry

-Third Uncle/Brian Eno

-Querida/Juan Gabriel

-Il faut savior/Charles Aznavour

Popular Consensus

"You don't need a weatherman to know which way the wind blows" - Bob Dylan

Prologue

Sunday, February 25th, 2007

The Kodak Theatre was alive with energy as Martin Scorsese left the stage clutching his long overdue Oscar for Directing. The glamourous audience had been through a lot and after nearly four hours, the end was in sight. Only one award remained. But as Jack Nicholson and Diane Keaton made their way to the stage, there was a great amount of uncertainty as to whom would be taking home that last little Golden Boy.

Normally the film with the most nominations is the shoe-in for Best Picture, yet for the first time in Academy History, the top nominated film wasn't even in the running. Despite its impressive eight nominations, the long gestating adaptation of the hit Broadway Musical, *Dreamgirls* had failed to secure the most important one. Though *Babel* had the second most nominations with seven, victory seemed unlikely as it had failed to win a single award all night. It was truly anyone's race. Who would come out on top?

Would it be Clint Eastwood's year yet again with his Japanese language WWII film, *Letters from Iwo Jima*? What about, *The Queen*? The Academy famously love Brits. Or maybe the feel-good, *Little Miss Sunshine* would follow in the tradition of *Marty* and *Rocky* to become the little film that could?

Despite the three awards it had already racked up over the course of the evening (Editing, Adapted Screenplay and Director) few saw *The Departed* as a real contender. It was a genre picture, it was violent, and it was cynical. This was the same Academy that had only one year prior singled out the maudlinly hopeful, *Crash* for Oscar glory. Surely they wouldn't give their highest honor to a film that the director himself later described thusly:

> "It has to do with the nature of betrayal. The nature of a morality which, after 2001, has become suspect to me. I'm concerned about the nature of how we live, how we're living in this country and what our values are. This new kind of war is going to continue. Our children are going to inherit it. It's not going to be over with by the time we're dead. It's like a whole worldwide civil war. How does one behave in that context? What's right and what's wrong in that war? On the street level of *The Departed*, no one can trust one another. Everyone's lying to each other. It fueled me in a way. It got me angry, it got me going."

Based purely off the applause as Diane Keaton read the nominees, it seemed as though *Babel* might end up walking away the victor. But then again this is the Academy Awards, not Opportunity Knocks. Jack Nicholson didn't even wait for *The Queen*'s applause to die down before tearing into the envelope. Once it was open, everyone fell silent. Keaton seemed giddy with anticipation. Who would it be? After a moment to examine the contents (and with an oh-so-subtle grin) Nicholson proudly announced the winner.

Just like that, the delusional optimism of *Crash* was obliterated and the rage of *The Departed* reigned. And this was only the beginning.

*   *   *

The Oscars are no stranger to darkness (The Reign of Reagan/Bush ended with the double-wammy of *Silence of the Lambs* and *Unforgiven*) but even during times as dark as The Great Depression, World War II, and Vietnam, the movie that took home the Best Picture trophy at the end of the night, was invariably something either feel-good or harmless. One of the most glaring examples came in 1990 when *Driving Miss Daisy* won Best Picture and *Do the Right Thing* only received a screenwriting nomination.

The darkness nearly arrived in 2005 when the Best Picture slate included *Brokeback Mountain, Capote, Munich,* and *Goodnight, and Good Luck.* But as we alluded to earlier, The Academy opted to take the easy way out via the mirage of depth that is *Crash,* with its myriad tales of intersections, hyperlinks, and O. Henry revelations. They were able to temporarily delude themselves with a whole lot of sound and fury, which in the end signified nothing.

Many like to claim that Scorsese's Best Director win the following year for *The Departed* was "a gimme" for all the times he was passed over in previous years, but that doesn't address the win for Best Picture. They didn't have to give William Monahan's screenplay an Oscar. They didn't have to give Thelma Schoonmaker her third award for Best Editing. But they did. It was the most awarded film of the night. And even if these were all a means to show love to a respected Auteur, they sure picked a hell of a movie to do it with. And no such claims of favoritism can be made with regards to 2007's slate.

2007

By the time the Academy of Motion Picture Arts and Sciences announced their nominees in late January of 2008, seven Democrats and seven Republicans had already withdrawn from the Presidential Race which would eventually come down to John McCain v. Barack Obama. And the two issues that would come to define that election (the Troop Surge in Iraq and the Global Housing Market) were already topics of hot debate. Seven years of George W. Bush (and all that entails) can really start to weigh on the National Psyche. Is it any wonder that we ended up with *Michael Clayton*, *Atonement*, *No Country for Old Men*, and *There Will be Blood* as Best Picture Nominees? Oh, and *Juno* was also nominated.

Movies take a long time to make. Of course there are stories of Spielberg or someone cranking out a film in a matter of months, but for the other 99.9% out there (those who cannot simply will a Green Light into being) development can be a long and arduous process. The screenwriting alone can take months, if not years. Then you have to find someone to finance it, find a cast, and find a crew. Once you're in production there are still myriad tragedies (man-made and otherwise) that can befall your film. And then there's editing, test screenings, re-shoots, etc. By the time of release, a film that was once very, "of the moment" can suddenly be passé. So when a film is able to really resonate with the zeitgeist, it's sort of a miracle. When four out of five Best Picture nominees are able to achieve this, it's time to really step back and take a long, hard look at both the films and the world that spawned them.

Michael Clayton

Regardless of what André Bazin, François Truffaut, and Andrew Sarris would like us to believe, it is possible for a film to have more than one author while still functioning as a coherent work of art. Of course *Michael Clayton* is writer/director Tony Gillroy's film. One need look no further than the fact that it centers around the dogged pursuit of an ominous organization doing very bad things, to find parallels with the *Bourne Trilogy* that Gillroy had just finished writing that same year. His interests and obsessions permeate both works. But this is also George Clooney's film.

After transitioning from TV to film in the late 90's (and after a few misfires), George Clooney was able to enter the New Millennium as a bonafide Movie Star. As a such, he was no longer required to blindly accept any job that came his way simply to put food on the table. He could suddenly afford to be picky and choose jobs that jived with his interests and politics. And that is precisely what he did with Section Eight, a production company he co-founded with filmmaker Steven Soderbergh in 2001.

Through Section Eight, Clooney and Soderbergh were able to champion filmmakers they respected, help new voices get established, and package their own Passion Projects. For Clooney, this meant political films that both directly and indirectly addressed the wars, torture, and Crony Capitalism of the Bush Era. Some of these films he directed (*Good Night, and Good Luck.*) others he just produced and acted in (*Syriana*). The eight films he acted in at Section Eight really form the basis of what we think of as a, "George Clooney movie".

Michael Clayton was his final film for the company, and it was one heck of a note to go out on. The way the exultation of Michael's car ride at the end of the film is undercut by paranoia and unease is a perfect encapsulation both of an artist about to step out on his own with a new company, and of a Nation on the eve of an election.

Atonement

As the novel of <u>Atonement</u> was published nearly simultaneously with the events of 9/11, it's impossible to argue that this was meant as any sort of allegory for the 2003 Invasion of Iraq, but there are still some interesting parallels. Both narratives are littered with instances where history could have gone differently. If only Robbie had given Briony the correct note. If only the Bush Administration had taken the PDB about Bin Ladden more seriously. If only Briony hadn't incorrectly identified Robbie as Lola's rapist. If only Colin Powell hadn't insisted Iraq had stockpiles of WMDs.

Now of course it's silly to equate the lives of two, physically attractive, fictional Brits with the thousands of Military and civilian lives that have been lost during America's unending War on Terror, but it is undeniable that both stories are about traumatized/scandalized characters who think they have all the answers, making decisions that result in people getting killed. These are both stories about regret and accepting the consequences of one's actions. Briony attempts to atone through her writing. George W. Bush now paints portraits of wounded Servicemen and women. Neither effort brings back the dead, or even a limb, but it's something.

There Will Be Blood/No Country for Old Men

It's fitting that the two films that took the biggest swings at W were both shot in Texas. Marfa, Texas to be precise. The same place where George Stevens, Sr. did the location work for *Giant* a half-century before. Not only were both films shooting in the same town, they were shooting at the same time! One day of filming on *No Country for Old Men* was even interrupted by the *There Will Be Blood* crew testing out the oil derrick explosion in the far distance.

These two films form a yin and yang of The Bush Years. While they both contain elements of the other, one film is overwhelmingly preoccupied with greed, and the other with violence. They also both center on symbolic characters who represent those preoccupations. Anton Chigurh and Daniel Plainview are forces of nature who exemplify humanity's worst impulses, but most crucially, they are still humans.

Often with parables and allegories, it is easy to dismiss the moral because the characters are clearly constructs, invented to behave in certain ways, in order to impart a lesson. There is no element of free will. Anderson and The Coens were wise to make sure that their symbolic characters still retained some element of humanity.

In Plainview, this is exemplified by his need for human connection (both with HW and Henry), which he constantly suppresses with drink in order to continue his quest for wealth. With Anton Chigurh, it's the fact that he can be wounded. The scene of him performing field surgery on himself in the hotel room lets us know that he can in fact feel pain, and that he is willing to put himself through a great deal of it in order to accomplish his task. Such scenes sympathize otherwise unsympathetic characters. We cannot dismiss them as something "other" because we too have felt pain and yearned for connection.

It's like discovering that you and a serial killer love the same band. You now share something in common with an "animal". That's because they are not an animal. They are human and you are human. What they did was something that humans do. Humans can do all sorts of ghastly things.

Sure you can blame Government and Business for committing us to two wars that killed thousands, but Government and Business are not sentient entities. They are run by people. And even if we are not part of Goverment or Business, we aided and abetted them. We were so wounded and afraid after 9/11 that we allowed them to "shock and awe" women and children half a world away on the flimsiest of evidence. And if anyone raised the possibility that this was over oil? Oh well, gas prices are too high anyway.

Anton Chigurh and Daniel Plainview are not nightmarish because they are inhuman, they are nightmarish because they are all too human. To put it into psychological terms, they are our collective id, unregulated, run amok. Laissez-faire, right?

2008 and Beyond

While it would not officially win its Best Picture Oscar until February 2009, the die was already cast for *Slumdog Millionaire* on November 4th, 2008 with the Electoral Victory of Barack Hussein Obama.

Produced with George W. Bush still in Office and set a world away, this film was the perfect balm for America in 2008. With two wars raging and an economy collapsing, we were in desperate need of some "hope" and "change". Jamal was our collective avatar and his candy colored fantasy (set to a pulsing soundtrack) allowed us to dive into some serious "shit" (murder, torture, prostitution, etc.) and come out on the other end both victorious and unscathed. Who cares if it's 100% fantasy!? More than any campaign ad, this film screamed out, "Yes we can!"

Unfortunately this victory would be short-lived. Merely one year later, we found ourselves back in Iraq (no metaphorical stand-ins this time) with *The Hurt Locker*. Had we lived with War for so long that we no longer knew any other way of life? At least we got our first ever female, Best Director win out of it! But in our rush to leave The Bush Years behind the following year (combined with our nostalgia for The Clinton Years) we inadvertently allowed a fox back into the hen house.

After five years in the wilderness, following his ousting from Miramax, the back to back wins of *The King's Speech* and *The Artist* in 2010 and 2011 solidified the return of Harvey Weinstein as a force to be reckoned with. Thankfully this period would not last for long. But now we are in this sort of amorphous time where narratives have yet to form. Or will one ever form?

For the remainder of The Obama Years, The Academy felt like an organization being pulled in a million different directions. There's the self-congratulatory Academy awarding *Argo*. There's the respectable and socially responsible Academy awarding *12 Years a Slave* and *Spotlight*. And then there's *Birdman* saying...something? Of course this is also the period in history that gave us #OscarsSoWhite.

And what of The Trump Years? Ideally films inspired by these "interesting times" will already be out of date before they make it to the screen, but who knows? We need look no further than the *Moonlight/La La Land* Ceremony or the debate over whether or not *Get Out* was "Oscar Caliber" for evidence of an Institution at odds with itself. But then again, that's our world.

With the abundance of streaming platforms and social media networks out there, nobody is on the same page anymore about anything. There's too much to watch, hear, read, etc. And we will never catch up. And there will always be something new to get angry about. And there will always be another hill to die on. We will all be separate-together in our own little worlds that occasionally overlap like a Venn Diagram. And when every Democrat that you can think of decides to run in 2020, will we actually be able to collectively rally behind anyone? Let's hope so!

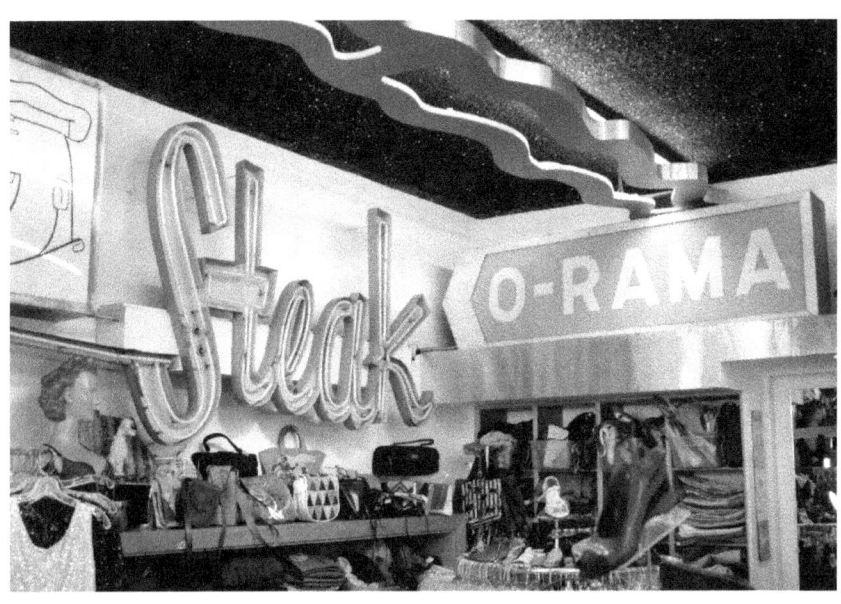

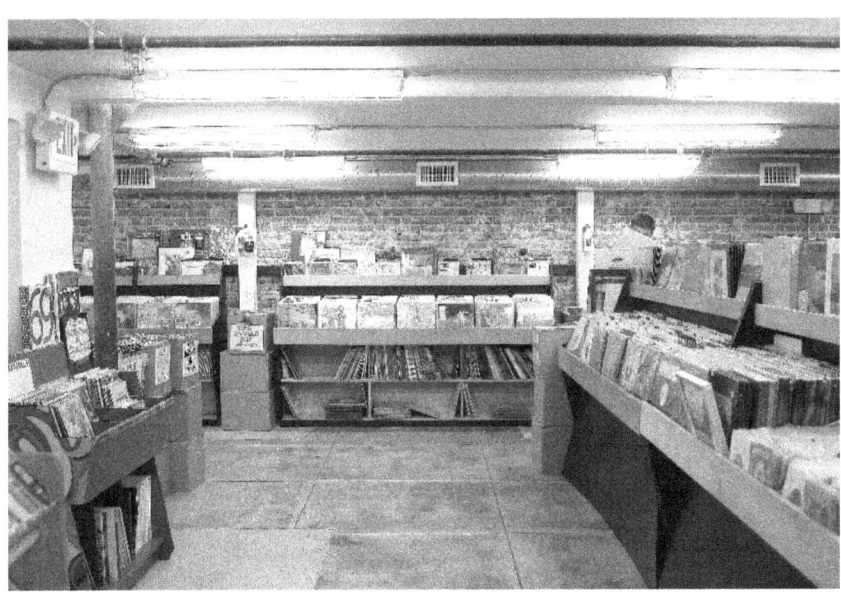

Playlist No. 23

-Across 110th Street/Bobby Womack

-Daves I Know/Bruce McCulloch

-Walking on the Moon/The Police

-White Light/Gorillaz

-I am a Cliché/X-Ray Spex

-Aphrodisiac/Bow Wow Wow

-Cleo/John Cale

-Hangin' 'Round/Lou Reed

-Needles in the Camel's Eye/Brian Eno

-We are Your Friends/Justice vs. Simian

-Do You Really Want to Hurt Me/Violent Femmes

-Livin' Thing/Electric Light Orchestra

Myself

Visual Acoustics: The Modernism of Julius Shulman

It wasn't until this most recent viewing (my third) that I really made the connection between architectural photography and film criticism. How did I miss it? Those are my two greatest passions! And it's all right there! At their most basic, both are creative endeavors that rely on someone else's creativity for a starting point. They're both about finding what is unique in a work and bringing attention to it in the most artful way possible. Both professions allow the artist to advocate for new talent as well as the old masters. Is it merely coincidence that a common term for having a particular "take" on a film, is to say that you have "an angle" on it? Julius Shulman was an amazing advocate for modernism and was able to transform that advocacy into masterful works that are able stand on their own. We should all strive to be that good at what we do.

mother!

It's insane that this film is being released by a major studio, on a ton of screens, and is being marketed as a horror film. I don't see this film making a dime over the weekend. People expecting a horror film will be disappointed and religious people will be enraged. But I couldn't help but giggle at the sheer anarchy of it all. It's scorched earth filmmaking that refuses to slow down once it gets going. Like The Poet, this film (and by extension Darren Aronofsky) craves your reaction and doesn't seem to care if that reaction is positive or negative. This film goes so for broke that it even prominently features a kitchen sink. It literally has everything AND the kitchen sink. I'm still grappling with what this says about me, but I simply cannot help but admire this beautiful, mess of a film.

Lone Wolf and Cub: Baby Cart in Peril

This film made me feel a very specific type of cinephile shame. Of the four *Lone Wolf and Cub* films that I've seen so far, I like this one best. So where does shame come into the equation? My shame comes from the fact that this is the first film in the series not directed by the legendary Kenji Misumi, who in addition to directing the bulk of this series, also directed six of the *Zatoichi* films. This is the one and only film in the series directed by Buichi Saito whose filmography is filled with films only an aficionado in Japanese cinema might recognize. I swear I'm not saying all of this to be a contrarian. I'm not trying to be "that guy" who prefers Lou Reed's Metal Machine Music to Transformer. I'm not even saying it is a masterpiece. Like the other films it suffers from not being able to successfully balance the ongoing story with the "adventure of the week". But thanks to Saito's particular use of pans, tracking shots and push-ins, my attention was maintained throughout the litany of endings. Perhaps I should track down more Buichi Saito films. Maybe I'll be the guy who "discovers" this forgotten master! Or maybe I'll just be that contrarian guy.

Chasing Amy

To many, liking the work of Kevin Smith is grounds for having your cinephile card revoked. Even I will concede that his most recent work (*Tusk*, *Yoga Hosers*, etc.) is near impossible to defend. But doesn't anyone remember those early years? Lately, I've been thinking a lot about *Chasing Amy*. Smith's tale of a hetero man who is unable to accept his girlfriend's fluid sexuality was more than a decade ahead of its time. Long before terms like "pansexuality" were able to enter the broader pop cultural lexicon via celebrities like Miley Cyrus or shows like *Broad City*, there was Joey Lauren Adams as Alyssa Jones delivering impassioned monologues about refusing to conform to what heteronormative society thinks is proper and insisting on loving whomever the hell she wants to love. Sure this message would have been more authentic and nuanced coming from a Queer filmmaker rather than from Smith, but because it came from him, it was able to reach a whole lot of immature boys who just wanted to hear dick and fart jokes. I know this because that's how I found my way to this film. I like to think that in some small way, *Chasing Amy* helped to move me towards becoming the ally that I try to be. And that's why I paid money to see *Cop Out* in a theater.

Ratcatcher

Since I recently became a father, I've been thinking a lot about motivation. I find myself staring at my daughter as she plays with her toys and I wonder how she decides what to do with which toys? What synapses are firing when she decides to smash two hunks of plastic together? What makes her suddenly decide to lick one item rather than another? Those same thoughts came to me as I was re-watching *Ratcatcher*.

At first I chalked it up to the fact that I am not Scottish and therefore am missing a lot of cultural nuance. But then there would be moments where Lynn Ramsay's camera is clearly suggesting that these characters don't know why they are doing things either. Why lie about not seeing someone's glasses when they are clearly right there? Why get on a bus when you have no idea where you are headed? Is all the trash around them affecting them like in an Antonioni film? So many questions and I love pondering every one of them. Such a beautiful film.

Little Men

I can't say for certain, but this film feels like it was directly inspired by Ira Sachs' previous directorial outing, *Love is Strange*. As much as I enjoyed that other film, what really stood out to me was that ending with the kids skateboarding. I can't remember too many specifics about the plot or even the characters, but those images of golden sunlight, long shadows and the overall feeling of hopefulness that accompanied them, finds its way into my brain fairly often. With its focus on the friendship of two young and openhearted boys, *Little Men* feels like it is intentionally picking up where that other film left off. The supporting characters of one film are now the leads of this new one. It's all so beautiful and subtle and perfectly honest about how the world works. A film this slight is destined to be forgotten among all the other great cinema of this year, but for me it is near the top.

I Fidanzati

Stylistically this film hits a real sweet spot for me. It's a perfect balance between the Neo-Realism of early Rossellini and the over-the-top stylings of late Fellini. It is a beautiful portrait of mid-century Sicily that relishes in the subtle details of day to day life, but with its very particular shot choices and radical cutting patterns, it is also extremely constructed. The leaps forward and backward in time, and the way they are tied together by the dancehall sequence is masterful and predates Nicolas Roeg by several years. And thanks to the "stranger in a strange land" narrative as well as the primarily silent protagonist, the digressions into the particulars of finding lodging and getting a late night meal do not feel extraneous. Ermanno Olmi is capable of making the extremely difficult seem effortless. For him, it probably was.

Everybody Wants Some!!

As much as I love Richard Linklater, I was a little bit dreading this movie. As if the branding as a "spiritual sequel" to the sacred text of *Dazed and Confused* wasn't enough, it was also going to be centered on a bunch of jocks! Was I going to willingly subject myself to two hours of frat boy antics? Much like a party where you don't know anyone, it took a little while to get into the groove, but once I found that groove I was hooked. And that's really what this movie is about: throwing yourself into different situations and adapting. It really reminded me of my high school experience floating between all the various cliques and enjoying them for what they were rather than what they were not. Like life, this film is about gobbling up experiences. You'll be surprised how much you have in common with people because, as the title states - everybody wants some!!

Tank Girl

Of all the various low/mid-budget comic book movies of the 90's (*Ninja Turtles, The Crow, Spawn, Blade, Barb Wire,* etc.) I think *Tank Girl* might be the masterpiece. Sure it bombed. The audience for the comic was so minuscule that I'm not even sure why someone shelled out money for the rights. And even the super-indie fans of the source material were put off by the Hollywood co-opting of their culture. So then why am I calling this a niche masterpiece? Because to a whole generation of weirdo kids just discovering punk, indie and DIY, this was the film pointed the way. It's a crash-course in collage-culture. Complete with a Cole Porter musical number and a whole bunch of bad-ass women to look up to/fall in love with.

West Side Story

As a kid I hated musicals. I hated *West Side Story* in particular. Why is there an overture? Why are they dancing? None of this is realistic! I loved *The King and I* when we watched it over the course of several rainy recesses, but that's Siam, in the distant past! For all I knew it was a documentary. *West Side Story* is about gangs! I saw gangs all the time on the evening news. Gangs don't dance. Gangs certainly don't snap. Where was the grit? Sure the songs were catchy, but it wasn't realistic!

It wasn't until many years later that I came to appreciate how sometimes, emotional realism can trump visual realism. To an outsider the Jets and Sharks might seem like a bunch of punk kids making the neighborhood a less safe place to live. But to them, the few city blocks which comprise their turf is a kingdom. To them it is epic. And that is precisely what the entire team behind *West Side Story* got right. The colors, sets, costumes and camera moves were all perfectly matched to the romanticized way in which these kids see their world. Everything is life or death and there is only Tonight. And damn if it isn't gorgeous.

The Wanderers

Seeing as *The Right Stuff* and the 1978 incarnation of *Invasion of the Bodysnatchers* are two films that I hold in extremely high regard, it's a wonder that I waited so long to see the film that Philip Kaufman made in-between those two. But it's also a kind of hard film to track down, so sue me! Anyway, though it comes nowhere close to the perfection of its predecessor and descendant, it's quite a good little picture. You can see elements of *Bodysnatchers* in a particular chase scene and the plotless focus on charismatic lunkheads clearly presages the Gemini astronauts of *The Right Stuff*. Sure things peter out a little after the second act climax, but it wins you back pretty easily. All in all it's a fun movie with a few actual thoughts on its mind and it deserves a wider audience. Perhaps the $49.99 price for the DVD on Amazon is holding people back? You can get the disc from Netflix. But like The Wanderers themselves, DVD's are a remnant of a bygone era that just doesn't know that it's time has passed.

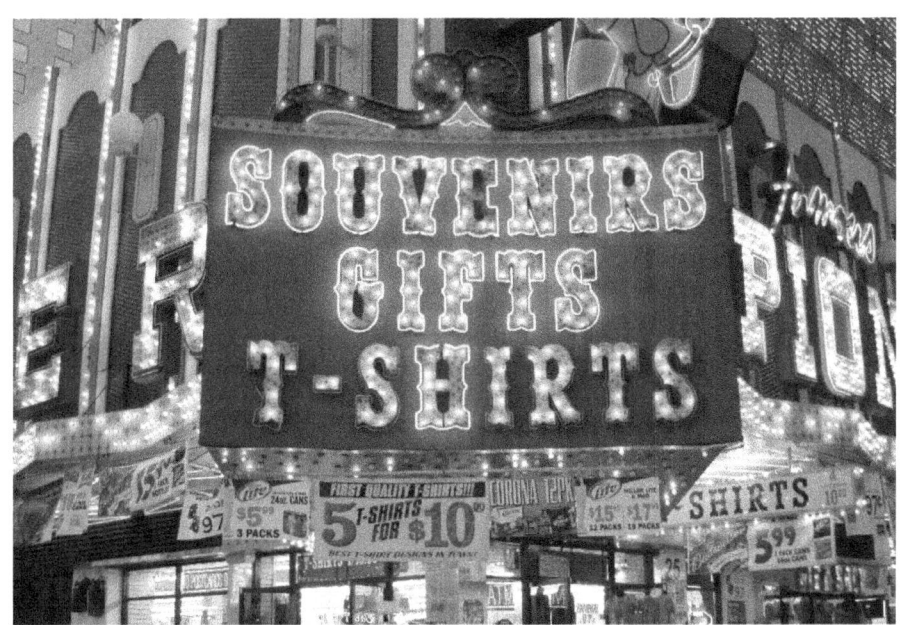

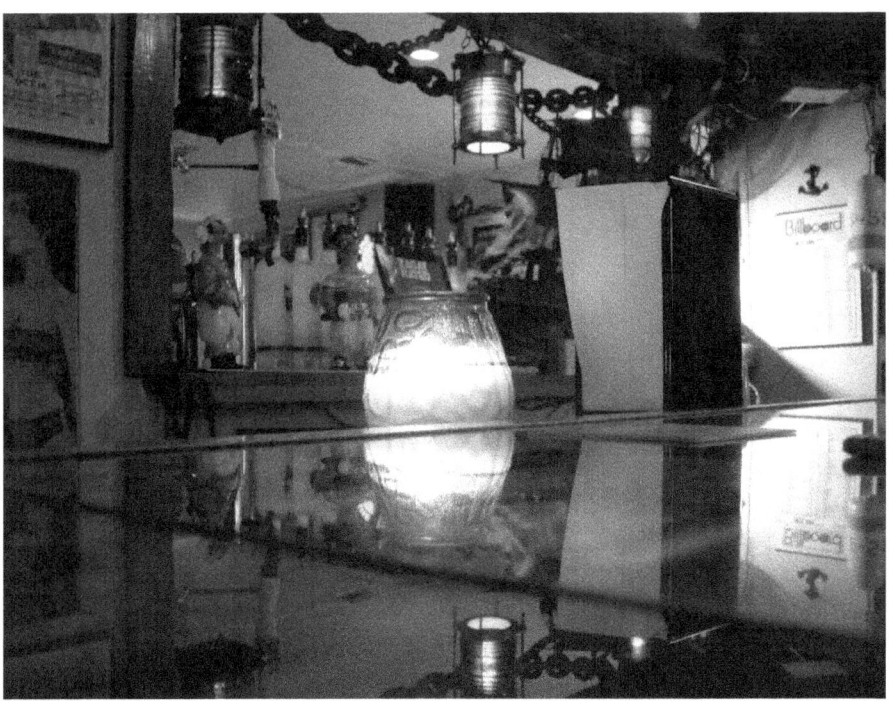

Playlist No. 29

-American Woman (David Lynch Remix)/Muddy Magnolias

-This is Hardcore/Pulp

-My Queen is Harriet Tubman/Sons of Kemet

-Rated X/Miles Davis

-Ladyfingers/Herb Alpert & the Tijuana Brass

-Rum-Dee-Dum-Dee-Dah/John Barry

-Danny's Inferno/The Three Suns

-You Want the Candy/The Raveonettes

-Brand New Key/Melanie

-My Sharona/The Knack

-Round and Round/Ariel Pink's Haunted Graffiti

-Dancing on My Own/Robyn

Films

Best of Cinerama

The first Cinerama production was titled, *This is Cinerama*. But it might as well have been titled This is Cinema because the roots go that deep. The five films compiled to make *Best of Cinerama*, bear a stronger kinship to the medium's pioneers than they do to Ford or Hitchcock. Part documentary, part travelogue, part amusement park ride, these Cinerama productions feel like the logical successors to the short curiosities and one-offs that the Lumiere Brothers and Edison trafficked in. Can't make it to The Louvre to see The Mona Lisa in its natural setting? Cinerama has you covered! Not tall enough to ride a rollercoaster? Cinerama has you covered! This is Cinema at its most elemental. This is Pure Cinema. And it is glorious.

Dunkirk

Remember the early days of IMAX when the theaters were mostly in museums and pretty much exclusively showed educational spectacle and documentaries? This kinda reminds me of those days. More so than anything else, this film is a visceral experience. When the screen is large enough to fill your entire field of vision it's hard not to get sucked in. But it's full credit to Christopher Nolan that it works this well. This could easily have been something along the lines of those weird attempts at doing narrative film in Cinerama. And it doesn't reduce human tragedy to mere spectacle either. *Dunkirk* is a uniquely cinematic experience. It almost seems sacrilegious that this will eventually be screened on televisions and phones. There's really only one way to truly see this film.

Pina

There are very few films that deserve to be filmed in 3D. I can probably count them on one hand. This one absolutely belongs on that list. I'm so glad I didn't settle for watching it in 2D. In other films, dance is merely about motion. Here I kept thinking about sculpture. You see every muscle and really understand what it physically takes to perform these pieces. And it's not just filmed theater either. As trite as it might sound, Wenders' angles make you part of the dance. Hopefully one day I can see this projected on a big screen.

The Director and the Jedi

I feel like I've lived through so many eras of home video. Not just VHS, into laserdisc, into DVD, into Bluray, into streaming, but also the different eras of bonus content. There was the early days of audio commentaries, trailers, and production notes. Then came deleted scenes. Then came electronic press kits. Then came the glory days of in-depth documentaries, branching modules, etc.

Since the public at large has overwhelmingly turned away from physical media, you're lucky to get a trailer on most releases. But now that digital services like Movies Anywhere have begun including bonus features, I'm optimistic that there might be another glory day ahead. People haven't stopped liking bonus features and studios will never stop needing to make you interested in their new technologies. It's a perfect storm from which we will only benefit.

The Director and the Jedi is one of the best behind the scenes docs I have seen in a long, long time. Hopefully it is the beginning of a trend.

Landline

On a plot level, I don't exactly get why this film was set in the 90's. The title makes you think that perhaps a shared phone line will play a crucial role, but it doesn't. This film could have easily been set now with no problems whatsoever. Our world is so obsessed with the past that all the 90's fashion and music could be used as well. So why set it in the 90's?

My theory is that director Gillian Robespierre made this film as a Tarantino-level genre homage. Only instead of homaging exploitation flicks from the 70's, Robespierre was paying homage to New York movies of the 90's. Dana is living in a Nicole Holofcener film a la *Walking and Talking*, Ali is living through *Kids*, and their parents are a Woody Allen film incarnate. And just like in *Pulp Fiction*, the supporting character of one story gets to be the star of another story.

It's a cool idea that never beats you over the head with showy visuals or title cards spelling everything out for you. It also doesn't attempt to elevate the material. This film is right on par with the films it is paying tribute to. This is a warm and funny film that is content to be adequate, and that is wonderful.

BlacKkKlansman

I know Godard and Tarantino are the directors most often held up as examples of filmmaking as film criticism, but Spike Lee is no slouch either. It's no accident that *BlacKkKlansman* opens with a clip from *Gone with the Wind*. Of course Lee's prime target is White Nationals and the President who has emboldened them, but NYU professor Spike also has his sights set on film history itself.

It makes perfect sense that back in film school, Lee made a short about a black filmmaker being hired to remake *The Birth of a Nation*, because *BlacKkKlansman* serves as a perfect inverse to D.W. Griffith's Klan-glorifying epic. Whereas the older film reinvigorated a once dormant hate group, Lee's joint is aimed at ridiculing that same hate group, and depicting them as the racist terrorists that they are. The most brilliant stroke is that Spike uses Griffith's own weapon against him - crosscutting.

Lee and his editor, Barry Alexander Brown, weave together a tapestry of parallel actions that leave poor D.W. in the dust. They cut between characters, cut between locations, cut between time periods, between fiction and documentary. They even cut between their film and Griffith's!

You can have quibbles about the film's possible glorification of the police, or the ways it plays fast and loose with "real" events, but thanks to Lee and Brown's skill with montage, there is no way in Hell you will come out of this film with even an ounce of respect for White Nationals. There are no "fine people" to be found there. And that's the triple-truth, Ruth!

Moonlight

On his audio commentary track for *The Graduate*, Mike Nichols seems rather proud of the fact that he was able to open the film by stating his theme outright. His pride is justified. It's tough to do. Usually the line where a theme is stated will stick out like a sore thumb and turn many people off. Oh, that's what they want me to think?! Only truly skilled directors like Nichols are able to pull it off. And the newest filmmaker to join that club is Barry Jenkins.

Not only is Jenkins able to get away with stating his theme outright, he's able to do it while also mentioning the film's title at the same time. That's just asking for trouble! But it works. When Juan tells Little about the Cuban woman who told him that, "In moonlight, black boys look blue" you don't exactly know what to take from that. Sure there's the double-meaning of blue as a color and blue as an emotion, but is that really all there is to this film? Is it just about sadness?

For me, the most important aspect of this film is light. This film is filled with different types of light. There is natural light, there is artificial light, there is direct light, there is diffused light, there's warm light, cool light and even highly stylized, colored light. And because this film is nuanced, everyone gets to be seen in a variety of those lights because no person is any one specific thing. In one light they are loving, in another they are hateful. The light can change from scene to scene or angle to angle depending on the emotion of the scene. Sometimes the light can even change within a shot.

So yes, black boys do look blue in the *Moonlight*. But that's just one type of light.

Marjorie Prime

So apparently this was a play before it was a film. I wonder if it had music when it was performed? I feel like the music is such a part of the whole and really made the movie for me. While it deals with big issues like technology and memory in a thoughtful manner, *Marjorie Prime* is very much a melodrama - in the Victorian sense. Mica Levi's beautiful score (and the few source songs) inform, overwhelm, envelope, and enhance the images. It feels almost like a silent film where a modern score was placed overtop. The music expresses that which is being withheld. It speaks for those who choose not to, and gives emotion to what we are told is just a series of 1's and 0's. Days later I'm still thinking about it all. Can't wait to revisit and dig deeper.

Possessed

In film school we learned a lot about the "classical Hollywood style". The central tenet of this "style" was to create a seamless experience where the audience is continuously enveloped in the story, and great pains are taken to preserve that illusion. Edits and camera movements are placed very strategically so that you do not notice them. While I'm pretty sure it was unintentional, throughout this film I was repeatedly made aware that I was watching a deliberate construct.

Right near the opening you have Joan Crawford walking down real Los Angeles streets, then you cut to her walking up to and into a restaurant that is very obviously a set. And then there are camera moves like the POV shot of Joan being wheeled into the hospital. Nothing seamless about a shot like that. Even the ways in which Crawford is lit to maximize her Joan-ness is a bit distracting.

When you later find out that her character is sometimes unable to distinguish reality from fantasy, I started to wonder if the clashing of styles was deliberate. Was director Curtis Bernhardt subtly preparing us for later reveals and shocks? Was he making a comment on the inherent falseness of the cinema? Judging by his filmography, I'm thinking not. But I love when a work of art allows my mind to roam to such places. That's what makes movies great. You can have your own little theories about them, like how *The Shining* was Kubrick's way of telling us the truth about the Moon Landing...

Hidden Figures

I really think this movie benefited from being seen in a theater. Not because of any sort of visual or aural grandeur. In fact, both those aspects of this film are pretty rote. What this film benefits from, is following a slew of awful trailers. I always dread seeing PG-rated films because all the trailers have to be family friendly as well. It's just this unending stream of platitudes and fart jokes. So the fact that *Hidden Figures* is actually good feels like a small miracle. Sure there are still scenes where smart people explain things to other smart people so that the audience can get the information, but oh well. The charisma of those three leads could get me through most anything. And they did it all without dirty words. No wonder my parents loved it.

Barcelona

So many filmmakers fall on their faces when making their second film. Emboldened by the success of their debut, most budding auteurs decide it is time to swing for the fences. Since many of these filmmakers have already said all they have to say with their first outing, these films are usually savaged by both critics and audiences. Whit Stillman's *Barcelona* should be studied in film schools as a model second feature. It's much more ambitious than its predecessor, but not embarrassingly so. It looks a lot like the last film, but is different enough to not be considered a retread. A second film is not a destination, it is just the next step in a journey. You don't have to do it all at once. It's OK to take baby steps and hold on to some things for later. Your sophomore film should be a detailed portrait of who you are at that precise moment in time. It isn't about where you think you should be. Perhaps you'll be able to do those ideas more justice when you're in your forties...or even your eighties!

Queen of Katwe

I'm not sure if it's due to the popularity of TV where there are A, B, C and D plot-lines to follow throughout a narrative, but modern films tend to have way too much going on. This is how we end up with Superhero films that run nearly three hours. It's also how we get a cascade of different endings that have to be resolved after the big bad guy has already been dispatched. Though *Queen of Katwe* is far from a straightforward story that is over and done with in 90 minutes, it does take the novel approach of resolving all of its lesser plot-lines before concluding the main one. This way, when the movie is over, it is over. I desperately hope that screenwriting courses will start teaching this as a way to more delicately handle all of that cinematic bloat.

Desert Hearts

I'm pretty sure that the idea of "love at first sight" was invented by a writer. As someone who has attempted screenwriting, I can tell you definitively that it takes a lot of pages to make characters believably fall in love. Love at first sight is a shortcut that allows the filmmakers to get to what they were really trying to make a film about. But what if your film is entirely and exclusively about the slow dance of falling in love? That is what *Desert Hearts* is. It's a short movie, but it takes its time building that love story. Like Cay, it is single-minded in its pursuit. Everything else just falls away. The whole world falls away. All that is left is the beauty of the desert, and these two women, falling in love. You really have to admire the simplicity.

Dracula's Daughter

I know we're all supposed to hate formula, but there's something comforting and liberating about it. I'd never seen *Dracula's Daughter* before, but knowing it was a sequel to a Universal Horror Film, I mostly knew what to expect. I could expect to see the same sets from the original film repurposed. I knew to expect an interesting array of character actors with distinct faces to distract from the lack of a "star", and I knew to expect the rather bland heroes. I knew it would take place in some odd time period that both is and is not the 1930's. Most importantly, I knew that this film's very existence would rely upon some wild retconning in order to explain the continuation of a story that was meant to be done with. So yes there are formulas and limitations, but it also requires the filmmakers to get wild and silly in order to make it work. That's how you get to Dracula's bi-sexual daughter who wants to put an end to her hunger and to settle down with a man for eternity. It's both progressive in subject matter and regressive in approach to that subject matter. Or is the film's conclusion a refutation of the Countess' desire to change? Or is the fact that she was (presumably) once human a way of saying that it's possible to "make" people queer? Lots to chew on in a 71 minute movie.

Doctor Strange

While narratively it's your basic origin story that we all know chapter and verse, what kept me engaged throughout this film was the visuals. And I'm not even talking about the special effects. Of course they were amazing and deserving of their Oscar nod, but what I'm really talking about is the overall look of the film. This is the first time since the original *Iron Man* that I actually gave a damn about how a Marvel Movie looked.

On that first outing for Marvel Films, it was all uncharted territory. As daring as it was for the studio to go with Jon Favreau as director and Robert Downey Jr. as star, it was also daring for them to go with Matthew Libatique as DP. Prior to *Iron Man* he'd only done extremely "in your face" films for the likes of Darren Aronofsky and Spike Lee. Choosing Libatique served everyone well in that they were getting a cinematographer who would make sure that their film looked nothing like the (then) recent DC films *Batman Begins* and *Superman Returns*. He helped Marvel to stand out from the pack...and then they got cold feet.

Every Marvel Movie since has been pretty much the same. You could splice them all together into one film and you wouldn't really notice when things switched from *Winter Soldier* to *Age of Ultron*. They found a "house style" and they've stuck to it, which I guess is fine, but the imagery in these films seems more indebted to Cinema than to Comics. These movies look like other films you might find in a multiplex. Except for *Doctor Strange*. This film actually looks like a comic book. And at certain moments it even looks like the kind of day-glo poster you would buy in a Head Shop.

Maybe their unending string of hits has made them cocky and Kevin Feige is finally loosening the visual reigns because he feels they can do no wrong? Or have these movies become something akin to a Woody Allen film, where the style is SO set in stone that the minor variations scream out for attention? I guess we'll just have to see how the next few installments look. Here's hoping for a little more variety.

Valerian and the City of a Thousand Planets

Black Holes are not visible. They are so dense that even light cannot escape their gravitational pull. We know that they are there because we can see all the stars and such that orbit them. Black Holes are the void at the center of intense cosmic beauty. Dane DeHaan and Cara Delevigne are the void at the center of this film's cosmic beauty. Their relationship drama is DOA, but all the set pieces, alien creatures, and space diplomacy swirling around them is truly something to behold. And fortunately, that's what most of the film consists of. It's pretty easy to check out for their Soap Opera and check back in for some universe-spanning wiz-bang. I can only imagine what it looks like on a giant screen.

Lights in the Dusk

This film feels like it was made on a dare. It feels like the type of challenge Lars Von Trier would lay down in *The Five Obstructions*: make a Film Noir - without guilt.

Unlike a traditional Film Noir, where the world is working against the protagonist as some sort of self-fulfilling, guilt manifestation, the hero of this film is guilty of nothing. He doesn't even have an opportunity to become guilty. People are hating him from the very start and for no stated reason. And it's not even some Kafka-esque exercise in paranoia because our hero is oblivious to all the ways in which people are conspiring against him. He's also equally oblivious to the few people out there who give a damn about him.

So is this Film Noir? No. But it is an Aki Kaurismäki film. And that's certainly something to savor.

Princess Cyd

While it isn't about gay cowboys eating pudding, this is very much what people think of when they think of an indie movie. It has female protagonists, it deals with trauma, it features bisexual and gender non-conformist characters, it's multicultural and there are prolonged discussions about fascinating/important issues. This could have felt like a bunch of topics or issues being checked off of a list. Instead it is one of the best films of last year. The characters are so well-drawn that you cannot help but care for them, and the whole thing is directed with the perfect balance of beauty and unobtrusiveness. I'm so glad to have finally caught up with it.

Appropriate Behavior

When this movie came out, that still of writer/director/star Desiree Akhavan sitting on the toilet was all over my tumblr feed. And then there was the poster with her staring at the straight, kissing couple. The moody photography of these images combined with the bisexuality and the whole Iranian aspect had me pre-judging this film in all sorts of ways. And while this film is about all those things, it's also really damn funny. Why didn't they play up that angle? For some reason they sold this film like NyQuil when it's actually Dimetapp. This film is bubblegum amoxicillin. I guess I would have been just as reluctant if they had played up the comedy. Could you imagine a poster with a rainbow flag on one side, an Iranian flag on the other side and Shirin in the middle looking quirkily confused? When a film is one dimensional it's fine to pick an angle and stick to it like glue. But when a film is as unique and nuanced as this one, you're doing it a disservice by making it out to be just one thing. Or maybe going in with pre-judgements helped me to like this movie better. Maybe I liked it this much because of all the ways it defied my expectations. Well, either way it's a good movie. You should see it!

Alien

I don't know if it's the bluray transfer or what, but while revisiting *Alien* for "Alien Day" I found myself continually in awe of what a visually beautiful film it is. I've seen it numerous times on VHS and DVD, yet here on bluray I came away thinking that it might possibly be one of the most visually perfect films of all time. Perhaps even moreso than the much more famously designed *Blade Runner*. Everything just feels so much of a piece with everything else. The Giger designs, the sunless lighting and the robotically clinical camera moves all work so well together. It's the aesthetic equivalent of the xenomorph itself, and apparently I am Ash.

> **Ash:** You still don't understand what you're dealing with, do you? Perfect organism. Its structural perfection is matched only by its hostility.

> **Lambert:** You admire it.

> **Ash:** I admire its purity. A survivor... unclouded by conscience, remorse, or delusions of morality.

10 Cloverfield Lane

In an era full of bloated crap that doesn't know what it is about and exists primarily to set up sequels and spin-offs, it's refreshing to find a film that is so narratively clear. Even though this movie is somehow related to *Cloverfield*, that doesn't change the fact that it is also an insanely well-structured film. It plants ideas and plot points that pay off in rewarding/surprising ways and most importantly - it is actually about something! Thank God the direction and acting don't get in the way. In fact, both those aspects are insanely strong as well. This film was a wonderful treat that can be enjoyed beyond the mysteries and spoilers. If they're able to keep up the same quality and clarity, I would gladly see more films in this universe.

Hero

It's interesting comparing this to American-made, big budget, historical epics. This was China's stab at something like *Pearl Harbor* or *The Patriot*, where money is not an object in helping to bring history to life. Of course it leaves us in the dust. Maybe it's because Yimou Zhang was directing, but this actually feels like a film rather than just spectacle. For all the lavish sets and costumes of *Gone with the Wind*, I have no clue what that film is actually about. This film is about something and has a message to impart about world affairs. And it's not some generic message either like "all's well that ends well". But perhaps to a Chinese audience the "message" is "old hat" and I just see it as profound because it's not American. ¯_(ツ)_/¯

Kill Zone 2

God I love Hong Kong Cinema! I know I'm showing my Eurocentric roots when I say this, but sometimes I forget that it exists. Back in the 90's it was EVERYTHING, but then something new comes along. Suddenly there's a new flavor of the week. But things don't just go away because you stopped paying attention. Lots of 90's bands are still touring with loyal followings. The same goes for Hong Kong Cinema. It is still alive and kicking, kicking, kicking. It's even keeping alive the old exploitation model of taking a popular title, slapping it on a new movie and filling it with stars from all around the world. It's comforting to know that Hong Kong Cinema will always be there for you when you need it. Go enjoy your mumblecore or whatever people are into these days. When you need to watch some serious ass-kicking, Simon Yam et al will be there waiting for you to catch up with everything they've been doing since you left. And unlike Matchbox 20, they've learned a few new tricks since the last time you came around.

The Purge: Anarchy

It's funny how much slack I will cut a film that doesn't take itself seriously. I can't stand the way Christopher Nolan's *Batman* films co-opted ideas like mass surveillance, terrorism, the occupy movement, etc. as a way to appear smart when they aren't actually saying anything at all. Fanboys love to hold these themes up as an example of why *The Dark Knight* should be considered serious cinema. *The Purge: Anarchy*, on the other hand, has no delusions about what it is. It's an exploitation thriller, pure and simple. And like the exploitation films of yesteryear, it is taking the "hot topics" of the day and using them as a hook to get butts in seats. It isn't trying to say anything profound about income inequality. It just wants to tell a fun, tense, action-filled story. I'd respect Christopher Nolan a whole lot more if he would just cop to the fact that his *Batman* films were doing exactly the same thing.

Train to Busan

There's just something inherently cinematic about trains. From the Lumière Brothers' film of one arriving, to Edwin S. Porter's *Great Train Robbery*, to the Cinerama splendors of *How the West was Won,* and beyond, trains and moving pictures have been inextricably linked. It makes sense. If you're making a movie, you want things to move. Also, the continuous forward motion mirrors the driving narrative of a well-told story. And let's not forget the fact that trains also make stops.

Sure this train is headed to Busan, but there are plenty of stops to make along the way, and it's these stops that help give the viewer some variety. And not just variety of location and action either. This "horror" film makes protracted stops at the "family drama" station, the "teen romance" station, and the "slapstick comedy" station on the way to its conclusion. At one point it even becomes an extremely current allegory for the plight of refugees. This movie gets that the journey is just as important as the destination.

Baby Driver

This film would pair nicely with *Collateral.* Beyond the fact that it allows Jamie Foxx to play the flip side of the role he had in the Mann movie, *Baby Driver* deepens the themes of that other film by having a much more engaged protagonist.

Baby isn't an innocent who chanced into this life by having the wrong person get into his car. Sure he owes Doc a debt, but it was boosting a car that got him into that position to begin with. He's a thrill seeker who wants none of the consequences. And this film is all about consequences. It's not about action v. inaction. Baby is already a man of action. But does he have the strength of character to live with those consequences once the dominos start falling? Or will he continue to drown out any unpleasantness with catchy R&B tunes?

Manhunter

Back in the early 30's, Universal was riding high on the backs of horror films like *Dracula, Frankenstein* and *The Mummy.* While none of these films were set in a specific time period, it clearly wasn't the 1930's. These were stories set in exotic locales or in "the old world" where the same creepy castle set could be used over and over again. And then Edgar G. Ulmer adapted Edgar Alan Poe's *The Black Cat* and decided to transport it to an extremely modern, art deco mansion. By setting a story of Satanic mutilation in such an orderly and sterile setting, the horror was amplified rather than diminished. This is exactly what Michael Mann does with *Manhunter*. Say what you will about the awful, faux-deco that was so popular in the 1980's, but the red of human blood really stands out on all those white walls and duvets.

The In-Laws

New York in the 70's was such a distinct cinematic creature. So distinct that John Carpenter had to wait until 1981 to have Snake Pliskin escape it. The colors, the fashion, the photography and the trash unite so many disparate films. No matter the production designer, you can't help but imagine *Taxi Driver*, *Shaft*, *Annie Hall* and *The In-Laws* all occurring in the same shared universe. It lends an air of gritty realism to even the wackiest of premises. So much so that when Sheldon and Vince make it down to the fictional island nation of Tijada, with its wacky general and singing soldiers, you're already completely on board. It just fits. The real and the absurd butting heads with each other to generate absolute hilarity.

The Terminator

It's really weird going back and revisiting this one. Especially in a post-*Genisys* world. It blows my mind that a film made for less than $10 million has spawned four sequels that each cost a MINIMUM of $100 million. And it's not like the original looks more expensive than its budget. It looks exactly like its budget. It looks like every other low-budget, high-concept action film of the time. You can tell what is a miniature and what is matted in. You can tell when it switches from a dummy to a real person. You especially feel it when Arnold is going to visit the first Sarah Connor from the phone book. It's just a guy in a big jacket walking up to a suburban house and you can picture James Cameron just out of frame in shorts and a t-shirt. I'm not saying any of this to put the film down. In fact, it's rather inspiring. There is really no magic to movie making. Just do it!

Far from the Madding Crowd

I wonder if there's anyone out there in the world still trying to make films in the Dogme 95 style. I'll assume that since there are people out there who still listen to Smash Mouth and Sugar Ray, the answer is yes. But like late 90's beach-rock, the Danish "vow of chastity" wasn't meant to last. It was merely a pallet cleanser for two filmmakers who had grown bored with shooting traditional coverage. And I guess it worked since both of those filmmakers are presently producing better work than they were before they took and abandoned those vows. Like Luke Skywalker, they had to unlearn what they had learned. Hopefully the intrepid souls out there who are still trying to get their films certified aren't debut filmmakers. I guarantee that you'll never get to a film as exquisite as *Melancholia* or *Far From the Madding Crowd* if you start your career with handheld non-genre films.

Listen Up Philip

Just as the Dogme 95 gang had to leave behind the affectations that united them in order to move on to more ambitious work, so too must the Mumblecore kids. But it's not easy. There is safety in numbers. This is why most will cling to that group label like a safety blanket as they go about re-making the same film until they die...or the money dries up. Striking out on your own means you might fail, but you gotta shake things up if you want to stand out from the pack. And it doesn't have to be anything big either. You don't need fancy cranes and computer effects. With a movement like Mumblecore it's possible to distinguish yourself with elements as simple as narration, score and good-looking cinematography. And this is why we know the name Alex Ross Perry and we don't know countless others. He has the daring to be maximalist in his minimalism.

Wendy and Lucy

This feels like the type of movie a lot of filmmakers aspire to make. They want to tell a small story with low stakes that focuses on the characters rather than the plot. Of course this is a lot easier said than done. Big stories and intricate plots exist for a reason - they draw people in easily! When all you have is a few characters in a fairly unremarkable setting you have to work a lot harder. I guess it also helps if you have an adorable dog as one of those characters. But that's not to take anything away from Kelly Reichardt who makes you viscerally feel every single dollar Wendy has to spend. Decisions about how to spend your last few dollars are just as important as decisions that involve the fate of the world. It's nice to see that somebody gets that.

Marie Antoinette

Though I never hated this film, I've really warmed to it over the years. It's a boldly subjective take on material that many find as boring as...well...a history lesson. This film has no interest in the political. It is 100% focused on the personal. Sofia Coppola's sole aim is to put you in Antoinette's fabulously ornate shoes. How long is a carriage ride from Austria to France? Long! How fun is a masquerade ball? As fun as grooving to Siouxie and the Banshees. And in spite of all the decadent decor and fashion, the camera work is pretty unobtrusive. With the soft, natural light, much of the film feels like home movies...from Versailles. And that final shot of the smashed chandelier is a thing of absolute, heartbreaking beauty. No chyron needed. We know how this ends. It all came crashing down.

Swiss Army Man

Going in, I assumed that this was going to be a film about making due with what you have and how desperation can lead you to questionable decisions. I expected an unintended parable for how the Republican Party is currently lashing themselves to the putrid corpse that is Donald Trump. And while I guess that reading could still stand, there's more to it. It's also a Ferris Bueller/Cameron Frye or Tyler Durden/Jack story about having someone to push you out of your comfort zone. It's also a story about farting. And about admitting that you are the one who farted. Just as Daniel Radcliffe's corpse was able to become whatever Paul Dano needed in the moment (be it jet ski or confessor) this film can also be a multitude of things. Why does it have to be just one? Though it never quite worked for me on an emotional level, I was absolutely impressed by how much mileage Daniels were able to get out of a simple premise. They squeezed out all that they possibly could.

Little Women

Adapting classic literature can be challenging. In addition to the normal problems that come with adapting a novel, there is the added complication of the fact that lots of early novels were pretty weirdly structured. Though the "hero's journey" is as old as time, I'm pretty sure Louisa May Alcott was not consulting Aristotle's Poetics as she was crafting her touching tale of the March Family. From the limited research I've done, the novel we think of as Little

Women is actually the fusion of two shorter works. In spite of all of this, the adaptation that director Gillian Armstrong, writer Robin Swicord and editor Nicholas Beauman were able to put together is pretty great. They were able to successfully include numerous, smaller, side stories from the book(s) without losing the overall thrust of Jo's journey of actualization. It is somehow simultaneously loose and tight. Few films are able to hit that sweet spot so squarely. It should be studied in schools.

Girlfriends

So crazy seeing a Warner Brothers logo at the head of a film this structurally daring and visually murky. Looking into the fairly limited amount of trivia about this wonderful movie, I discovered that Stanley Kubrick was quite the fan, and it makes perfect sense. Though it has little in common with the aesthetics and themes Stanley trafficked in, Vicki Polon's structure is very Kubrick.

Rather than telling a conventional story, *Girlfriends* is a collection of moments that build upon one another. Long spans of time elapse between scenes and the audience is trusted to figure out where we are. Each scene builds upon the last while also being its own contained moment. The ending is cumulative and satisfying without that contrived/inevitable feeling that accompanies most traditionally structured screenplays. While there certainly isn't a straight line between *2001* and *Girlfriends*, you can see a circuitous kinship.

Edge of Seventeen

Before this movie even started I was already baffled by the sheer number of company logos at the start. Had the trailers been hiding something from me? Was there going to be some effects-filled, third act twist that would justify so many funding sources for a film about a teenage girl trying to figure her life out? Not to spoil anything but, giant robots and dinosaurs do not show up at any point in this movie. So why did a hilarious and heartfelt film, produced by a Hollywood legend, starring an Oscar nominee who also appears in a popular franchise, need to go to so many different sources for such a modest $9mil budget? I'd venture it has something to do with the fact that the director was a first timer...and female. Please pay to see this film and show all those financiers that their money was well spent!

Speed Racer

With a budget of $120 mil, *Speed Racer* might be the most expensive art film ever made. Like the *Matrix Trilogy* and *V for Vendetta* it has a lot on its mind, only this time the Wachowski's want you to really listen. They're using bright colors and willfully unrealistic CGI in much the same way that Bertolt Brecht used harsh lighting and spoken stage directions to alienate the audience and make them aware that they are being messaged. Like Godard they are taking the conventions of pop cinema and turning them against the audience. There is no way you can walk out of this film and not be thinking about corporate greed, good CGI v. bad CGI, and studio filmmaking. Even 12 year olds are certain to come out of this film a little more woke than when they went in.

Black Sun

This was an interesting one. It reminded me a lot of a Sam Fuller movie, in that it is the cinematic equivalent of performing surgery with a sledgehammer. It's blunt and it's pulpy, but that doesn't mean that it can't get at some tough and interesting truths. The truly interesting part about this film is the language barrier. This isn't a movie where people have to talk out their differences, because neither speaks the other's language. All they are able to go off of is tone, facial expressions and body language. And somehow they come to understand each other like one does a jazz song or a silent film. Perhaps the Tower of Babel was not meant to separate us, but rather to force us to unite on a deeper, more human level?

Paddington

Wow! That was extremely pleasant. I'd been hearing people sing this film's praises for years, I just didn't believe them. I kept thinking back to that trailer, which is just the entire "facilities" scene. Who chose that scene to lead with? It's not really that representative of the film as a whole. Were they just hoping to appeal to the lowest common denominator? Probably. It's a shame though. By taking the easy route, you miss out on audience members who might appreciate how sweet the film is. Or miss out on people who prefer more nuanced or absurdist humor. Or people who aren't six-years-old. Hopefully the sequel doesn't drop the ball. I promise not to judge it by its trailer. I'll trust you guys this time!

The Fits

As someone who writes about movies, I am constantly trying to "get" what I have just seen. What are the filmmakers trying to tell me? Did it come across? Could it have been stated more clearly? But not all art is meant to be "got". Some art is meant to be experienced. Some art is just there to give you thoughts and feelings. It isn't trying to tell you what to do with those thoughts and feelings. If they wanted you to take a message away from the film they would have written an essay. Instead, they chose to use cameras and actors and sound and editing to make you feel something. And just because it's art, doesn't mean that it is boring. I hope the fact that it is unrated means that adolescents are getting the chance to see this. It will show them that movies can be anything. And so can they.

Neruda

The best films are films that could not exist in another medium. If it can be written as an essay, it should be an essay. If it could be staged as a play, then it should be staged as a play. I don't know if I simply lack the skill or insight, but I cannot seem to put into words what *Neruda* is doing. I understand it and it provokes fascinating thoughts in me about art and politics, but there is no way I could ever rightly put them into words. It would be a bunch of scattered thoughts with no center. Perhaps Pablo Neruda could have done it. Pablo Larraín certainly did it with this beautiful film.

Rumble Fish

What a difference a lack of color makes! Stylistically and thematically, there isn't too much distance between this film and *The Outsiders*. They're both highly-stylized gang stories that make extensive use of camera tricks and opticals. But for some reason, *Rumble Fish* doesn't make me want to claw my eyes out. You'd think that the lack of color would draw even more attention to the stuff I hate, but instead it transforms ludicrous things into gorgeous ones. Black and white transports this film to another world entirely. *Rumble Fish* is 100% artificial and I love it for that. As Coppola stated, this is an Art Film for teenagers. Sure it's R-rated, but it's a pretty soft R. Why can't substitute teachers show THIS Hinton adaptation to their classes? It's guaranteed to ignite adolescent imaginations and we need more of that.

Time Bandits

As much as I've enjoyed a number of Terry Gilliam's films for grown-ups, this rewatch of *Time Bandits* has be convinced that his true calling is making imaginative films for children. The slapstick comedy, manic pacing, and Fellini-esque visuals are perfect for getting and keeping a child's attention. This film in particular is also just dangerous enough to entertain adults while simultaneously fooling kids into thinking that they're getting away with something. Even Gilliam's messages, which are a bit too simplistic to be taken seriously by intellectuals, are just deep enough to be considered profound by your son or daughter. Of course these films also tend to be a touch overlong, but that's just a tiny quibble compared to the large-scale pleasures at play. It's a shame that J.K. Rowling wasn't able to get him to direct one of the *Potter* films like she wanted.

Krampus

Since the PG-13 rating was created in reaction to *Gremlins*, a part of me has always felt that PG-13 films should be aimed at the same audience as *Gremlins*. The PG-13 rating is a stop-gap between childhood and adulthood and the films made with this rating should reflect that. It's perfect that some parents/critics bristle at what makes it into a PG-13 film. That's what this rating was made for. It's made for teenagers. It's made for kids who are just starting to enter a scarier, sexier and more nuanced world and they want their films to reflect that. You can only shelter them for so long before you're actually doing harm. *Krampus* is a perfect PG-13 movie. It is ideal for a middle-school sleepover. It's also great for making adults feel like they are that young again. Watch it this Christmas on a double-bill with *Gremlins* for the full effect.

The People under the Stairs

Not too long ago I was writing about "ideal" PG-13 films. These are movies that are perfect for middle schoolers to watch at sleepovers. They push the content boundaries enough to make kids feel grown up without getting too violent or sexy. But where do you go from there? Do you go head-on into *Cannibal Holocaust*? Perhaps? But there can also be a step in-between, and I think *The People under the Stairs* fits the bill perfectly. In a lot of ways it should be PG-13, with its insanely over the top adolescent POV, but there's also just enough language and gore to make that rating a no-go. If *Krampus* is a film for 6th graders, this is a film for 8th graders. Leave your copy somewhere that your kid can easily "borrow" it and think they're getting away with something.

Female Prisoner #701: Scorpion

As Michael Bay can surely attest, an over-abundance of style can easily paper over a great many deficiencies. If it's flashy looking, you won't notice the cardboard characters, plot holes and dubious politics because you are being constantly bombarded with spectacle. But style can also help distract from the fact that you do not have a budget. Pretty much all of *Female Prisoner #701: Scorpion* takes place in one location and good chunks take place in a large dirt field, yet it is one of the most visually inventive films you will ever encounter. Even something as subtle as a colored light can make something cheap look interesting. The participation of a leading lady as magnetic as Meiko Kaji also helps too. I'm really excited to see where this series goes!

Stray Cat Rock: Delinquent Girl Boss

Oh man! Where has this series been all my life? It's so alive with cinematic energy! Like Steven Soderbergh with the *Ocean's* films, this film is willing to try anything to get your attention. Color, music, editing, swinging cameras - nothing is off-limits. One gag leads to another and before you know it the movie is over and you had a great time. It's ludicrous that a film this wild was able to be made by the same studio that had just fired Seijun Suzuki for being too wild. Perhaps they were too preoccupied with Suzuki's lawsuit against them to really know what was going on? Who knows! I just know that I can't wait to check out the rest of this series!

Stray Cat Rock: Machine Animal

Since all five of these films were released within eight months of each other, you can't really say that they factored in the audience's responses to the previous installments, but it kind of feels like it. *Wild Jumbo* tried doing something wildly different from *Delinquent Girl Boss* by having a mostly male cast and then in *Sex Hunter* they seem to have learned that the less men the better. Gratefully, *Machine Animal* seems to have learned from *Sex Hunter* that loads of rape tends to undercut your political messaging. They even seem to be addressing it with dialogue before the opening brawl. Watching these filmmakers and actors actively figuring out what does and does not work via trial and error is a very interesting experience. I have only one film left in the series. Will it be the masterpiece where everything truly comes together? Probably not! But that doesn't mean this hasn't been a pretty wild and enjoyable ride so far.

Stray Cat Rock: Beat '71

I was a little nervous going into this final *Stray Cat Rock* film seeing as it was directed by Toshiya Fujita who also directed the series low-point, *Wild Jumbo*. Why not finish it out with series-starter Yasuharu Hasebe who directed all the other entries? Thankfully all my fears were for naught. While not the out and out masterpiece of *Lady Snowblood* (which Fujita would go on to direct two years later) *Beat '71* is a solid film and also a fitting end to this weird little series. There's a lot of loaded imagery in that final battle where Eastern Culture is literally doing battle with Western Culture - in a Wild West Town no less! Perhaps for others this will come off as heavy handed, but for me, when you throw in the reprise of that Mops song and those poetic closing images of Maabô, cinema doesn't get much better.

Mississippi Grind

Much like the film's protagonists, I thought I knew where this was heading. While they had visions of wealth and happiness, I foresaw only misery. In the end we were all pleasantly surprised. From moment to moment the conclusion vacillates wildly between triumph and tragedy. If it ends at one moment it is a story of the American Dream realized. If it ends at a different moment it's a story about that inner hole that can never be filled. So, where does it end? Which moment does it end on? That depends on you. It's a cinematic Rorschach. Is the glass half-empty or half-full? You have to know how to read the tells. And even if you're great at it, you could always be wrong.

Christine

In the past I've admired films "based on a true story" for taking us inside of private moments that a documentary never could. This film I admire for keeping us outside.

Throughout the runtime, we are presented with all sorts of reasons why Christine might have done what she did. There's her physical health, there's her mental health, there's her home situation, her love situation, her work situation, and of course there is also Watergate. But when it comes time for her to do the deed, we still have no clue why she did it. Perhaps it was a combination of all the things we've seen. You can comb through hours of tape looking for an answer, but the only person who can truly give you that answer is dead.

To try and place an answer on to Christine's actions would be doing her a great disservice. Rebecca Hall's performance deserves far more recognition than it has received thus far. She compassionately honored a woman who, like so many other women throughout history, has been reduced to just a single thing.

Tower

Who would have thought that a movie about a massacre would be the film to leave me with a renewed faith in humanity? I certainly didn't! While most films would focus on the shooter and his motives, this film hardly makes, mention of him. This isn't a case of plastering one of the Boston Bombers on the cover of <u>Rolling Stone</u> like he's some sort of rock star. I'm not totally certain, but I feel like they don't even say the Austin Shooter's name out loud, and the only photo of him is as a baby. This is a film about the victims, about their lives and their experiences. It is also a film about compassion, sacrifice and even forgiveness. Oh and it's a cartoon too. Man I love cinema!

Canoa: A Shameful Memory

I really appreciate how this film takes its time. It appreciates the importance of building to a climax. But it also appreciates the importance of a good tease. That opening where the reporter is taking down the bare bone facts of the story is a master stroke. It satiates the impatient viewers by letting them know where things are headed, while also building a sense of dread into every moment that follows. There are no happy scenes because we know what is to follow. Innocent questions of who will stay and who will go are imbued with life or death stakes. Even unintended things like the priest's glasses and that PA system give unintended dread by conjuring Jonestown two years before it even happened. Movies don't get much more horrific. And it is all true.

Z

Man that ending still packs a wallop. When I first saw this film a few years ago, it took me by absolute surprise. In a Trump/Brexit World, it's a painful reminder that sometimes the polls are wrong. Sometimes the bad guys win. There is no reassurance to be found here.

They say that films where the characters hold back tears are more likely to elicit tears from the audience. Here, Costa-Gavras is holding back Revolution in hopes that it will inspire the audience to start one. "Any resemblance to actual events, to persons living or dead, is not the result of chance. It is DELIBERATE."

Rogue One: A Star Wars Story

People like to make a lot of noise about the *Star Wars* Universe's roots in myth, legend and pulp fiction, but there's a flip side to that coin that is often forgotten - the series' roots in revolution. Like the rest of his draft minded generation, George Lucas was steeped in the politics of Vietnam and his student films *Freiheit* and *Electronic Labyrinth THX1138 4EB* vividly reflect this in both style and substance. Yet by the time he got around to crafting his little Space Opera, all the messy politics of a rebellion were pushed to the background so that a story of family and succession could take the fore. Even the aesthetics were sanitized to purely functional storytelling. *Rogue One* goes a long way to restoring balance to The Force. Here we get a rebellion that is split into factions and far from a united Front. Here we get protagonists who have no qualms about killing someone who might draw unwanted attention. Here we get a film that owes a visual debt to *The Battle of Algiers* and the cinema of Costa-Gavras. It's far from perfect, but in a universe so preoccupied with cycles and repetition, it is a welcome breath of messy air.

Southside with You

I can't remember what podcast it was on, but a while back I heard someone doing a bit about how only the most well-known black people get biopics (*Malcolm X*, *42*, etc) while any-old white person can get one (*Joy*, *Flash of Genius*, etc). That bit kept cycling through my mind while I watched *Southside With You*. This is that premise stretched out to a ludicrous degree. Do you think this film would have been made/admitted to festivals if it hadn't been about the then-current POTUS and FLOTUS on their first date? Richard Linklater has made three films like this about random, fictional, white people. But this one had to be about the early years of the First Family in order to get Sundance attention. That's some bullshit.

The City of Lost Children

In many ways this feels like the last truly great international film. Watching the opening credits I found myself constantly remarking, "Oh man, I forgot [so and so] was in/worked on this film!" David Lynch's composer! Woody Allen's future cinematographer! The director of *Catwoman*! And of course, Ron Perlman as One. It's also fitting/subversive that Jean-Louis Trintignat is being used exclusively for his voice when that voice was famously dubbed over in oh so many Italian films. This is the kind of co-production you used to see all the time in the 60's and 70's, but I can't really remember the last time I saw anything of this level in recent times. Maybe the failure of *Alien: Resurrection* and the aforementioned *Catwoman* caused producers to get a little gun-shy. Oh wait, I just remembered the career of Timur Bekmambetov. So I guess I'm full of shit. Still, this film is a great example of people coming together from all over to make something awesome. I want more of that!

The Lobster

I'm not sure if it began this way, but *The Lobster* really feels like a satire of YA dystopian films like *Divergent*, *The Maze Runner* and *The Hunger Games*. Of course this one stars middle-aged schlubs, but all the signposts are there. There are rules, there are factions, there's a color scheme and of course there's intense oppression. Yet, instead of playing these elements for strained seriousness and tired "insights" that we've seen countless times over, Yorgos Lanthimos and his collaborators play them for extremely bleak comedy. Just try to not laugh at the fact that bisexuality is no longer an option and that shoes don't come in half sizes. And rather than diminishing the impact, this deft approach miraculously enhances the insights that the film makes into human behavior. It may be a comedy, but the laughs really stick in your throat.

Five Came Back

This was an interesting experience. Since I had already read Mark Harris' excellent book of the same name, a lot of these stories were old news to me and that really held me back in the early chapters. I mean it was cool getting to see some of the footage that I'd only read about, but nothing new was really brought to the table. There wasn't anything that really justified this being a film rather than a book. But then there's that final third. In its final hour, this doc really becomes cinema. As fascinating as I found the book, it didn't move me. The final segment of this film moved me greatly. *Five Came Back* will go down as one of the finest documentaries about cinema ever.

One Day since Yesterday: Peter Bogdanovich and the Lost American Film

As a pretty serious movie nut, I have seen quite a lot of documentaries about film. Docs about specific films, docs about specific filmmakers, docs about movements, docs about techniques - I've seen them all. As edifying as most of these are, few of them actually rate as good cinema. Most of these docs come from a place of fanaticism and therefore the impulse is to include anything and everything that you can find related to your subject. This results in a long ramble that merely ends because there is no more material. What makes Bill Teck's *One Day Since Yesterday* so unique is that it actually has a shape to it. Rather than just being a big love letter to *They All Laughed*, Teck is able to place that film within the context of Peter Bogdanovich's greater life and filmography. There's a real arc to this film. You begin by learning about Bogdanovich before he met Dorothy Stratten, then you get to spend a long time on their relationship and learn about the lovely film they made together, and then you are there with Peter through his loss of Dorothy, and lastly you get to see the various ways in which that loss is still shaping his life and career. As the end credits will attest, there was a lot more material that could have been used in the body of the film, but wisely Teck chose to place his narrative and emotion first. The result is a satisfying and heartbreaking whole that all cinephiles should seek out as soon as possible.

Life Itself

If you know me at all you know that I'm extremely hard on documentaries. Paint by numbers does not work for me. Bio docs are often the worst offenders. If I wanted a list of incidents I would just read the person's Wikipedia page. While *Life Itself* certainly does make a point of checking off all the key moments in Roger Ebert's life, it stands out by choosing to mirror the structure of the biography on which it was based.

Rather than telling a strict chronological narrative, Ebert's book is structured much more like a series of essays where each covers a different aspect of his life. There's the one about journalism, the one about alcoholism, the one about Scorsese, the one about Chaz, etc. Instead of a simple list of accomplishments, you get to take in all the numerous and diverse aspects of Roger's life. He wasn't just a film critic. He wasn't just a recovering alcoholic. He wasn't just a TV personality. He was all those things and many more. This is a film about all the different elements that make up a person. This is a film about *Life Itself*.

Green Room

Now this is what I'm talking about! Unlike a lot of you, I did not care much for Jeremy Saulinier's last film, *Blue Ruin*. I didn't hate it, I just found it to be rather generic. Nothing really stuck with me after that initial viewing. I even find myself mixing it up in my brain with other films. Thanks to the specificity of the Punk v. Skinhead divide in this outing, there is no way that you could possibly mix this film up with any other. All the little nuances of those subcultures are handled just right. You get the significance of certain elements without having to have them turgidly explained to you and they add up to a more well-rounded experience overall. The more specific you get, the more universal you become. Also, who could possibly forget Anton Yelchin?

Zazie dans le métro

Browse any account of the French New Wave's beginnings and you're sure to encounter some variation on the idea that these filmmakers were reacting against "a certain tendency of French Cinema" which inordinately favored prestigious literary adaptations commonly referred to as "The Cinema of Quality". They counteracted this "tendency" towards "quality" by making highly personal cinema which flouted all of the accepted rules of both filmmaking and screenwriting.

At roughly the same time, Raymond Queneau was in the process of flouting all of French Literature's established conventions via his colloquially written novel, Zazie dans le métro. The confluence of these two contrarian movements was inevitable. Regardless of whether or not you consider Louis Malle to be an official member of the Nouvelle Vague, the sheer energy of the *Zazie* film is undeniably New Wave. From start to finish, Malle was able to expertly match all of Queneau's clever verbal wit, with equally inventive visual wit. Moreso than even the cartoonish satires of Frank Tashlin and The Marx Brothers, this film was absolute cinematic anarchy. *Zazie* was punk before there was a word for it. Vive Zazie!

The Florida Project

When Allison Anders was looking for a cinematographer to lens her film *Mi Vida Loca,* lots of candidates tried to impress her by talking about the "gritty" looks they were capable of getting. Anders opted for Rodrigo Garcia instead, because he recognized that the whole point of the movie was to be from the POV of Echo Park residents who see their neighborhood as the most beautiful place on earth. A quarter century later, Sean Baker and his team appear to have taken the same approach to their film - *The Florida Project*.

Just because the budget is small, the actors are non-professional, and the locations are functional, doesn't mean the film has to look like garbage. From frame one, *The Florida Project* has more style than 90% of the crap out there. Cinematographer Alexis Zabe and Production Designer Stephonik Youth are able to turn a couple motels and a few restaurants into a child's wonderland that is on-par with the amusement park around the corner. This movie can seriously stand toe to toe with *Killer of Sheep* and *Pather Panchali* as a romantically subjective depiction of impoverished living, featuring non-actors, that still bluntly acknowledges the brutality that can encroach from any and all directions. And then there's that ending!

How was this not a Best Picture nominee and *Three Billboards* was? This world is a cruel place. But it's also beautiful.

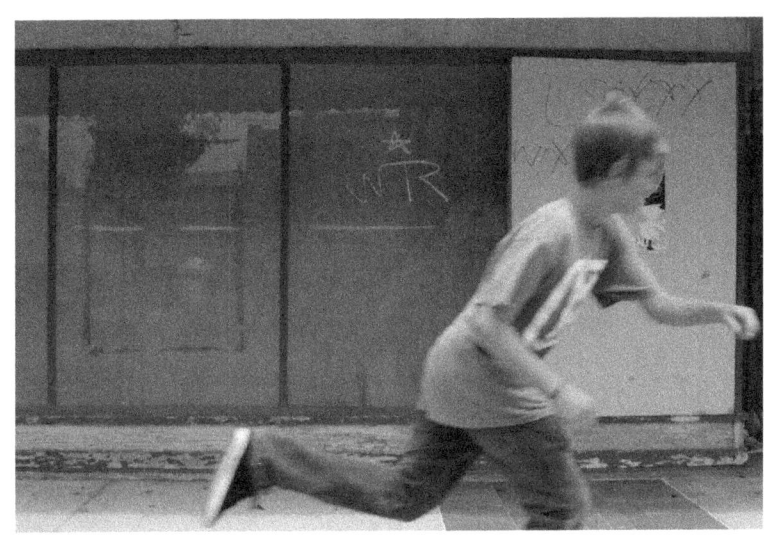

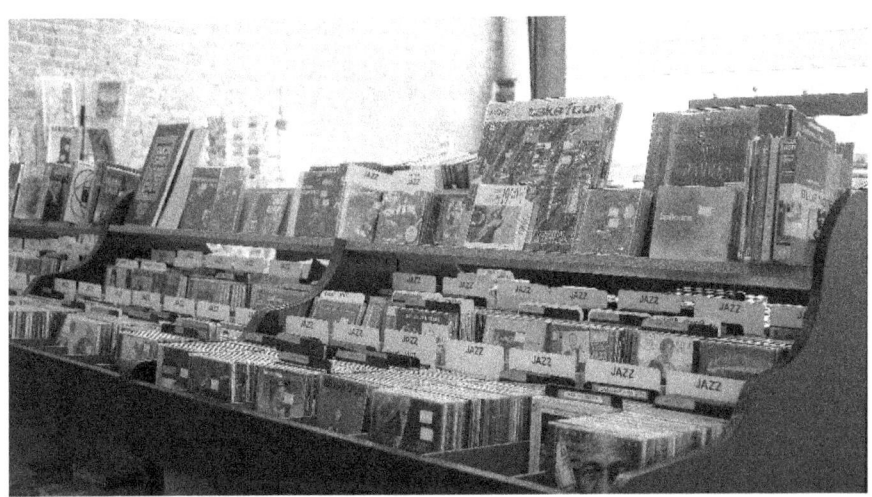

Playlist No. 34

-Going to a Town/Rufus Wainwright

-American Music/Violent Femmes

-Olita del Altamar/Café Tacvba

-Come a Little Bit Closer/Jay and the Americans

-Put the Blame on Mame (Slow Version)/Rita Hayworth

-El Paso/Marty Robins

-Bad Girls/M.I.A.

-Let's Talk Dirty to the Animals/Gilda Radner

-Valerie/Mark Ronson feat. Amy Winehouse

-Stormy Weather/Tommy Burk & the Counts

-North American Scum/LCD Soundsystem

-I Give You Power/Arcade Fire feat. Mavis Staples

Filmmakers

On Dangerous Ground

"Nicholas Ray is Cinema." - Jean-Luc Godard

I've been wrestling with that statement for the better part of two decades. Let me state up front that I don't dislike his films. I've seen six and have enjoyed them all. They're good pictures, capably told, and filled with immense sadness. But is that the epitome of Cinema? Ray is often revered for his use of the wide-screen frame, but to my eye, it's purely functional. Not bad, but functional. And what of the films he made before CinemaScope? But there is also no denying that he is an auteur. The sadness I spoke of earlier is uniquely his. It's there in all of the films I've watched so far: sadness and regret.

The more I reflect on it, Godard's statement was the mid-century equivalent of clickbait. Simply stating that someone is a good director who makes films you relate to was not enough! It was especially not enough in an era when genre films were thought of as trash and directors seen as little more than glorified traffic cops. Godard's hyperbole did the trick at the time and placed necessary attention on a serious artist. But is Nick Ray truly the be all and end all of Cinema? I don't think so. I don't think any artist can ever truly epitomize all of their medium's endless possibilities. If this was possible, what would be the point of any other mere mortal picking up a camera? Nicholas Ray is a very good director. Let's just leave it at that.

The Breaking Point

Michael Curtis is almost the perfect inverse of my issue with Nicholas Ray. While I find Ray's work to be filled with personality (ie: sadness) on a narrative level, I find his use of imagery to be only adequate. Curtiz on the other hand, has a gorgeous visual sense with nothing thematically holding his body of work together as a whole. And so, Ray is oft held up as an Auteurist God, while Curtiz is dismissed as a competent craftsman. They dismiss the genius of William Wyler and Robert Wise for the same reasons. And while I agree that their filmographies cannot be read like a novel, it's foolhardy to dismiss individual films for this reason alone. Andrew Sarris wrote of forests and trees, can't we have both? Why do they have to be mutually exclusive? I'd argue that the closing moments of *The Breaking Point* are bolder than most studio pictures of the era. I'm glad Criterion saw fit to bring it into the fold as a work that is worthy of attention.

The Shape of Water

A director's job is more than just coming up with wild shots. It is also more than developing a very deliberate color palette. A director's main job is to answer questions. This hat or that hat? Happy or sad? Faster or slower? The correct answer to any of these questions depends on the director's taste. Guillermo Del Toro is a director of exquisite taste. Like a master chef, he knows just how much of each ingredient to include in the dish. Just the right amount of comedy. Just the right amount of gore. Just the right amount of sex. On paper, *The Shape Of Water* should not work. In other hands, the story of a mute woman falling in love with a gill-man would induce ridicule and laughter. But under the guidance of a master like Del Toro, it is a front-runner for numerous awards. This is all thanks to Guillermo's excellent taste.

Rachel Getting Married

I'd been meaning to revisit this one for months. It's unfortunate that it took Jonathan Demme's death to get me to finally put the disc in the player.

Man he had such a big heart. You can feel it in every frame of his work. He loved people and he loved life. You can tell that he drank in every moment spent with another human and appreciated all the things that made them unique. And his concept of love was not a naive one either. He knew that life and love are complex and that things can get really dark at times. His light moments are all the lighter because darkness is still very visible in the rear-view and around the periphery. The cinema of Jonathan Demme is the cinema of forgiveness.

We have lost a great artist and (by all accounts) a great human. Rest in Peace, Mr. Demme. Thank you so much for all the beautiful and loving films.

Good Morning

Roughly 500 years ago, Leonardo da Vinci declared that, "Art is never finished, only abandoned." From apocryphal stories about artists breaking into houses to tweak the color of a painting, to George Lucas' continual futzing with the *Star Wars* films, it's been notoriously difficult for creative individuals to accept that a work is done. Even artists who have moved on from one particular piece, will often return to that style or those themes in another work as a way to get another bite at the apple. And of course there are directors who literally remake their own films.

Sometimes the results can be as astounding as Michael Mann's reworking of the TV Movie, *L.A. Takedown* into *Heat*. Other times the resultant film can be as awful as George Sulizer's English-language remake of his own chilling, Dutch-French co-production, *The Vanishing*. But most of the time it results in an enjoyable film that is no better or worse than its previous incarnation. Such is the case with Ozu's pleasant, family film *Good Morning*.

Phantom Thread

Though it was the Scorsese-like, visual gymnastics of *Boogie Nights* and *Magnolia* that caught the eye of the Film School Kids, we must remember that the principle influence on Paul Thomas Anderson's debut film *Sydney* (aka *Hard Eight*) was *Melvin and Howard*. Instead of opening with a whole lot of whiz-bang, both films begin with protracted conversations between two characters. At his core, this is who Paul Thomas Anderson is as a filmmaker.

Of course he played around with all the fancy toys on his next couple of films (who wouldn't?), but as early as *Punch-Drunk Love* you can sense a filmmaker casting aside all of the bravura in favor of a simpler, more character based cinema.

For all its fire and fury, *There Will Be Blood* is the story of three people in the desert. *The Master* is a love story between Freddie and Lancaster. Even with all the Pynchonian intrigue, *Inherent Vice* is really just the story of Doc, Bigfoot and Shasta Fey. *Phantom Thread* is Anderson's minimalism taken to its logical end-point.

It's not shot on antique, large-format cameras and most of it takes place in small rooms. It's not about Capitalism or Religion or any other "important" issue. The only maximalist element in the whole thing is Johnny Greenwood's wonderful score.

It's taken him many years and films to get to this point, but Anderson has successfully pruned away that which is not essential, held on to a few handy tricks, and returned to where he started. But this is no ending. This is a new beginning. And I cannot wait to see what comes next.

Fitzcarraldo

As I watched that boat inch up the mountain for prolonged stretches of real time, I found myself thinking about other, long in development "passion projects."

Martin Scorsese had famously been planning *Gangs of New York* for a quarter century prior to rolling film. And you can really feel it in the end product. Scorsese and his co-writer Jay Cocks had years to research and they wanted every bit of that research to end up on screen. That's how you end up with an extremely simple revenge story taking nearly three hours to unfurl. Though *Fitzcarraldo* didn't take twenty-five years to make it to theaters, it wasn't the easiest of journeys either.

Is Werner Herzog spending so much time on the practicalities of getting that boat over the mountain as a way to justify all the effort expended in filming it? On one level the answer is, yes. To simply throw away footage that took so long to amass would be insanely wasteful. But also, to abbreviate the scene would diminish what Fitzcarraldo and his comrades accomplished. The whole film is about struggle. To tell it in 90 min would be just as insane.

Fitzcarraldo's plan was an immense undertaking. Herzog's filming of that plan was also an immense undertaking. Shouldn't our experience of watching it also be an immense undertaking? And all of it in the service of bringing a little beauty into the world. Bravo!

Chimes at Midnight

Orson Welles is possibly the best and worst director for filming Shakespeare. Just as old Bill takes simple stories and ornaments them with elaborate language, Welles takes simple stories and ornaments them with elaborate camera moves. Both men love to juxtapose extreme bawdiness with deep emotion. And Shakespeare's extremely minimal stage direction gives Welles ample opportunities for invention. Much of the time this marriage results in beautiful images and moments. Most notably in the large battle at the center of this story. But it can also tip the scale in the opposite direction. When excess in language is piled upon excess in cinema all you get is indecipherable excess. It can sometimes become all too much. But when it works, it is beautiful. When you see the hurt in Falstaff's eyes near the end, many sins are forgiven. You get why this story was so personal to Welles.

Silence

Though he is easily the filmmaker most identified with Catholicism, in recent years Martin Scorsese has come to publicly self-identify as a "lapsed Catholic". So why make this film? He's famously been trying to make it happen for the better part of thirty years. If he were still a man of Faith one might understand the single-minded pursuit of bringing this story to the screen. Absent that, what could possibly have carried him through all the years, accidents and lawsuits? What else could engender that much devotion in a man? While I cannot say for certain, I feel that it was Scorsese's passion for the art of Cinema that kept this project alive for him over the decades.

For a while it seemed as though Scorsese had joined his peers in apostatizing celluloid by shooting multiple features digitally, and theatrical exhibition by working in television. He even directed a promo for a movie themed resort in Macau! Yet in spite of such seemingly heretical gestures, here comes *Silence*. At 161 minutes it is certainly not a YouTube video and the 35mm photography by Rodrigo Prieto is as gorgeous you might expect. It seems as though Padre Scorsese has not lost the faith after all. Like Catholicism, cinephilia is something that simply cannot just be given up. Despite many outward signs, it's always there, just under the surface.

20th Century Women

Though still (relatively) early in his feature filmmaking career, the filmography of Mike Mills has come to exemplify a fascinating exception to one commonly held truism about an artist's trajectory.

Like novelists, most directors tend to start their careers with an autobiographical work that is either about their childhood or their current romantic situation. Even the filmmakers who head straight into genre will undoubtedly still include a protagonist who parrots whatever he or she thinks about life, the universe and everything. Then, if that first film is good enough to be successful, it becomes imperative that the filmmaker does something different on their next go around. They have to turn their gaze outward at the wider world. Unless your name is Mike Mills.

With each successive film, Mills has opted to get more personal and to look deeper inward. Though he did not write the novel on which *Thumbsucker* was based, he clearly felt a kinship with its infantilized protagonist. As a follow-up, Mills dropped the surrogacy of adaptation and instead chose to make a film about his father's late in life coming out and the impact that had on his relationships with other humans. For *20th Century Women,* he's gone even further into the past to examine his relationship with his mother and the other women who shaped him.

Though each film is even more autobiographical than the last, rather than coming off as naval-gazey, the overwhelming feeling imparted by these films is one of intimacy. The more specific he gets about the granular details of these lives that are under examination, the more universal the overall work becomes. We might not be able to relate to the specifics of the narrative, location, time period, song choices, etc., yet I'm certain that somewhere in this film's lazy rhythms you will find something to love. Who doesn't love a great Annette Bening performance?

Lady Bird

Lady Bird had me thinking a lot about Claire Denis. I'm not sure what Greta Gerwig thinks about Ms. Denis' work, but the extremely brief, impressionistic scenes that comprise *Lady Bird* reminded me a lot of films like *Bastards, Beau Travail,* and *Trouble Every Day.* "Arrive late and leave early" seems to be Gerwig's modus operandi. She gets right to the heart of why we are being shown this scene or that scene. And as soon as she's made her point, it's on to the next little moment. She only lingers when it counts. She's sparing with these moments and savors them. After years spent on other people's sets she knows what she wants and knows how to get it. I cannot wait to see where she goes next.

Tully

I was rooting for Diablo Cody to win that Oscar for *Juno.* But as soon as she had it in her hand, I worried. Would this be as good as it gets? This was her first screenplay.

Would she turn out to be someone who didn't have anything else to say?

I've heard it said of musicians that you have your whole life to make your first album, and a year (at best) to make your second. With six features and a TV series to her name, I now feel safe in saying that Diablo Cody had more to say, and she will continue to have more to say. Perhaps stepping away from social media as she did has granted her more time to hone her craft rather than skating by on name recognition. More likely, that stepping back allowed her to live a life and that life is what's informing her work. Each project is a glimpse at who she is now. She is an evolving artist and it shows in her work, effortlessly.

Perhaps Jason Reitman should stick to exclusively directing her scripts. Because it seems that when he's left to his own devices, the effort to say something profound really shows.

Logan Lucky

If one were trying to describe the Cinema of Steven Soderbergh in a single word, "political" probably wouldn't be the first adjective to spring to mind. But if you look at his filmography, the overwhelming majority of his output has dealt with issues of class. Even his "sexy" movies (*Magic Mike* and *The Girlfriend Experience*) are first and foremost about commodification and wealth. So, while *Logan Lucky* appears to have sprung from the same mold as *The Cannonball Run*, it is first and foremost about Middle America. But unlike the first *Magic Mike*, it isn't cold and clinical. In fact, If I had to sum this film up in a single word, that word would be, "compassionate". And we could all certainly use a lot more of that in this day and age.

Okja

Last year, when we were polling readers and critics in order to make a new Pantheon of great directors, I really wrestled with whether or not to include Bong Joon-Ho on my own list. The decision to omit him is something that I think of often. Were I to be making my list today, after seeing *Okja*, I would absolutely drop Alexander Payne to make room for Bong.

Nobody out there today handles tone as deftly as Bong Joon-Ho. He can swing from tender, to crass, to horrifying, and back to tender all within the same scene. And it all feels like a unified whole. The current slate of Marvel and Star Wars films long to be this emotionally diverse. Hopefully *Okja* is a big enough hit to make someone who actually gives a damn about theatrical distribution put up the money for his next film. Bong's imagination is too large for the small screen.

Columbus

Can filmmaking be taught/learned? Being able to notice and appreciate the inspired techniques and motifs of a great filmmaker doesn't mean that you will be able to execute them yourself.

These were my thoughts going into the debut feature of visual essayist kogonada. And while he certainly didn't produce a masterpiece like *Tokyo Story* on his first at-bat, he did succeed at internalizing the techniques of Ozu et al and personalizing them. That *Columbus* doesn't feel like a Tarantino-esque stream of citations is a small miracle. He makes the experience seamless. You are not distracted by the style. He is not teaching. He is being.

Perhaps the next one will be *Tokyo Story*.

Monster

This film is much more than Charlize Theron's excellent performance. If this movie had been directed by a man, that director's filmography would absolutely be longer than two feature films in fourteen years. Patty Jenkins gets so much out of such a short runtime. AND SHE WROTE IT TOO! Meanwhile, people like Josh Trank and Colin Trevorrow are just handed millions of dollars after debuts with nowhere near the same tonal complexity as *Monster*. How Patty Jenkins didn't go on her own rampage during the past fourteen years is completely beyond me. Well at least Trank and Trevorrow got fired from huge gigs while she is gonna make a huge payday for the second *Wonder Woman*. Now if only we could get Hollywood to consider Ms. Jenkins as something other than a fluke...

Seven Beauties

I finally watched a Lina Wertmüller film! And now I want to watch ALL of the Lina Wertmüller films! Why did I wait so long? I really want to give The Academy credit for nominating this film for four awards including Best Director. I get that it thoroughly checks off that "holocaust" box that Oscar Voters love so much, but it does it in such an audacious and radical way. Or maybe I'm just observing things from the perspective of today. In the 70's, you could simply say that Nazis and Fascism were bad because they are bad. Today, saying such things will get you branded as Anti-Fa. Funny how a film can become MORE radical with age! And that's not even taking into account all of the gender issues at play here. Brava, Lina!

Cameraperson

Aside from a few moments of intense montage that draw parallels between seemingly disparate things, this is an extremely unobtrusive film. It is one sequence, and then it is another sequence, separated by black like it's an early Jim Jarmusch film. Each black screen cleansing the palate and clearing your mind of what came before so that you can better appreciate the next spectacle on its own. But can you truly forget what came before? Everything adds up. What came before shapes how we react to what comes after. And by mixing in home movies as well, Kristen Johnson also addresses the call and response between one's work-life and home-life. But it does this all in such a measured way. Thoughts come to you as you watch and you think that they are by chance, but Johnson intended you to have them. That's her hand pulling up a weed to create a better composition. She is the *Cameraperson* and we are seeing things as she sees them, so that we might share her thoughts.

Twin Peaks

When people talk about *Twin Peaks* they tend to talk about giants and little men who talk backwards. They talk about the Black Lodge and Owl Cave. And while all of those elements are very much part of *Twin Peaks*, they are not part of the pilot. Things don't start getting dreamy until episode three. But that doesn't make the first episodes any less Lynch.

What struck me on this rewatch was how reliant this pilot was on mood and inference. Right from that first close-up of the Palmer's ceiling fan. You can imagine executives imploring David Lynch to cut it out and keep things moving, but thank God he didn't. Things like that fan and the swaying traffic light are laying the groundwork for where things are going. They are the "acceptable strangeness" that prepares us for the truly dark places we are going to eventually find ourselves in. Just as Sarah Palmer and Donna Hayward are able to infer Laura's death before they are explicitly told, we too are able to read the signs and glean the greater significance of what is afoot under the small town surface.

In this pilot, David Lynch is giving us the keys to unlocking his and Mark Frost's weird little world. I can't wait to open that door again.

Inland Empire

On a recent re-watch of *Mulholland Drive*, I was observing how many scene transitions were simply hard cuts. One minute we are with one set of characters and the next we are with a whole new group of characters. We have no clue if they are connected but we go along with it. In-between those two scenes is where the cinema of David Lynch resides. We are shown one image and then another and it is up to us to make or find the connections and divine meaning.

Having been filmed in pieces over years, *Inland Empire* stretches that premise nearly to the breaking point. Lynch himself didn't even know he was making a feature until well into production. He'd come up with an idea for a scene and film it, then a few days or weeks later he'd have a new idea and film that. There was no finished script, the actors had no context of what came before or after. There's even an additional 90 minutes of unused footage this is available as DVD bonus material.

Unlike *Mulholland Drive* and *Lost Highway*, I have yet to hear anyone give a coherent "reading" of this film and I don't think it's really even possible to give one. It's an immense collage of pain and sorrow (garmonbozia?)

peppered with the occasional dance number. It's not a Disneyland ride with a narrative throughline. *Inland Empire* is one of those carnival spook-houses where shit just pops out at you. You don't wonder how The Creature from the Black Lagoon got to Transylvania, you just go along for the ride and have an experience.

Twin Peaks: The Return

Over on the *Twin Peaks* Facebook group that I frequent, I've jokingly asked how soon after the conclusion will we all disband and go our separate ways. While I'm sure many will leave and posts will become less frequent, I doubt any of us will stop thinking about *The Return* any time soon. There is so much to dissect and so much that is still open to interpretation. This series contains multitudes. It's a Joycean work so immense and thick with allusion that it is certain to launch a thousand academic ships. It's about film, it's about television, it's about America, it's about trauma, it's about men and women, it's about nostalgia, it's about aging, it's about death, it's about time. And of course there is that ending(?)

Making my way through this season has truly been a once in a lifetime experience. In this age of DVR and streaming services it feels like nobody is on the same page with anything. Everyone is doing things at their own pace resulting in few truly communal experiences. And while I know that most of the world wasn't watching, over these past months I have felt extremely in sync with so many people. And now that it is over we can watch it as one giant flowing whole that will certainly yield new insights. David Lynch and Mark Frost have bent television to their will and I am truly thankful for that. In fact they've bent it back so far that it isn't even television. We are like that first audience in Paris witnessing the The Lumière Brothers' first films unspooling before us. We are sharing a dream in the dark - awoken by a scream.

Gook

I've never quite understood why "...a filmmaker to watch!" has always been such a popular blurb for trailers and posters for films by up and coming directors. It implies imperfection. It implies that *eventually* this filmmaker will produce great work...just not yet. Perhaps they are hoping to appeal to those that like to proudly proclaim that they were into something before everyone else? Having acknowledged all of this, I find myself compelled to say that Justin Chon is a filmmaker to watch.

Sure this movie is tripped up by a last-minute jaunt into heart-wrending, message-imparting contrivance...but that's no reason to cast the whole thing aside. Everything leading up to that climax is just so damn wonderful. Chon excels at portraying a believable world, filled with fascinatingly flawed characters, informed by experience. The way he peppers in the TV coverage of the Rodney King verdict embues every scene with a sense of dread and inevitability. Even the decision to shoot in black and white, which could have come off as pretensious, instead comes off as a loving nod to the way that indie films looked in 1992.

The final act problems this film has aren't insurmountable either. A filmography is a learning process and this is only Chon's second feature. I cannot wait to see what lessons he takes from this and applies to his next film. Like I said, he's a filmmaker to watch. They'd be wise to leave that off the poster, though.

I Don't Feel at Home in This World Anymore

Just the other day I was telling someone that I'd love to see *Family Plot* (Alfred Hitchcock's flawed, final film about amateur criminals who get caught up with professionals) remade by the Coen Brothers. But if they're not available, I would now accept Macon Blair as a suitable substitute. The tone mixing in this movie is spot-on. It's like two completely different movies that dance with each other for a while before full-on colliding in the final act. The comedy makes the violence more intense and the violence makes the comedy more darkly hilarious. It's the cinematic equivalent of a Reese's peanut butter cup: two tastes that taste great together.

The Big Sick

As someone who listens to massive amounts of podcasts I was already extremely familiar with this story going in. Emily and Kumail's courtship is a cornerstone of the comedy podcasting world. They've told this story separately, they've told this story together, they've told it on other people's podcasts, they've told it on their own (now defunct) podcast. And that's just the number of times they've done it on mic. You know they've had to tell this story a million times at various social gatherings with friends and family. And then they wrote a screenplay about it. And then they got notes from Judd Apatow and Michael Showalter. Yet somehow this story did not become stale. I knew exactly where this was going and I was still hanging off of every word and scene. All that podcasting and such paid off. Like the great comedians they are, they honed this material into its ideal form. They know where the laughs are and where the tears are. They are able to play the audience like a fiddle. And they do it expertly.

Call Me by Your Name

I've seen lots of Italian Films in my day. From Neorealism to Giallo, I've taken in some of the best Cinema that boot-shaped country has to offer. Yet, as "sensual" as that country truly is, that is not the word I would use to describe their films. Luca Guadagnino is the exception.

Unlike his countryman Paolo Sorrentino, I don't feel a slavishly self-conscious debt to the operatic camera movements and emotions of Fellini, Visconti, or Leone. From the enveloping soundtrack of insects and wind through trees, to the sun-soaked photography that is so bright it warms you with refracted light off the screen, every artistic decision here is intended to make you feel as though you are actually in the north of Italy, in the early 80's, during summer. There is no need to beat us over the head with heighten emotions in desperate hope of making us feel something/anything. We are already/immediately right there. We are taking everything in with all five senses simultaneously. We can smell the sweat, taste the food and feel the caresses. We are living it. We are living the good times...and the sad times, too.

Coco

The other night 'Becca'lise was telling me about a coworker who was trying to guess why Coco is making everyone cry. Seeing as the movie is about Dia de Muertos, the coworker justifiably guessed that the big, tear-jerking scene centered on the death of a prominent character. If this was any other film, they would have been right. But this is a Pixar film. They never take the easy route. Yes a beloved character dies in this film, but at least in our theater, that passing was only greeted with a brief, audible sigh from the entire audience. No tears. Because in *Coco*, death is not an end. As long as someone is remembered, they are never truly gone.

Kubo and the Two Strings

Dead parents are so omnipresent in animation that it has become a cliché. It's a quick way to make you empathize with the protagonist while also presenting more opportunities to place that protagonist in harm's way. They have nobody to protect them and must therefore rise to the occasion and save themselves.

While Laika has mostly avoided this trope, death is still very much a presence in all of their work. It is most notable in *Kubo* and *ParaNorman*, but that morose atmosphere really hangs over all of their films. The closest cinematic parallel I can find is in the run of death-obsessed, horror films that Val Lewton produced for RKO in the 40's. Though Laika's films aren't so cynical as to subscribe to Lewton's sentiment that, "death is good." they are much more honest about grief, the various forms it can take, and the way we all live with it.

I know audiences didn't turn out for *Kubo*, but I'm optimistic that this will be the year that The Academy finally sees fit to honor this plucky, little studio for what I see as their masterpiece. This is the film where everything they do best comes together in the most satisfying way. It's a real bright-spot in a rather mediocre summer. Don't be scared off by all the crappy family film trailers that play before it.

I'm not there.

This film is a real Catch-22 because the only way to tell the story of a chameleon like Bob Dylan is to have the film change along with him...creating a fragmented experience that never really comes together as a cohesive whole. It's like a really great album with a few bum songs thrown in to knock you off balance. And I'm sure that really pleased Dylan. This is the man who willfully alienated most of his audience by going electric and by becoming Born Again. While some of the metaphors, allusions and homages help to bring us deeper into Dylan's mind, others only serve to alienate us further. The result is a film that's nearly as enigmatic as its subject. It will never be a perfect film, but it is absolutely perfect in its imperfection.

The Man who wasn't there

Somewhere among the masterpieces, the failures and the crowd-pleasers, this film tends to get forgotten in the Coen Brothers oeuvre. Even though it shared Best Director at Cannes with the newly ordained "Best Film of the Millennium" *Mulholland Drive*, *The Man Who Wasn't There* has become a bit of a phantom film. Sometimes I even wonder if it actually exists. But there it is on myself. It's almost too perfect that this film about an extremely passive and forgettable schlub, has itself become forgotten. And just like its protagonist, the film also holds surprising depth. That's the sort of extra-textual synthesis that you simply cannot plan. Or maybe the Coen's can?

The American Friend

This is an interesting one. It feels the most autobiographical of the Wim Wenders films I've seen. The cameos by Sam Fuller and Nicholas Ray, the dedication to Henri Langlois and the inclusion of early optical toys clearly indicate that Wenders wants us to be thinking about cinema itself. Viewed in this context, the forgery subplot seems like a knowing nod towards his early career, where Wenders himself acknowledges that his directing "style" consisted of little more than approximating Hitchcock and Cassavetes. Even the Zimmerman character agreeing to serve as a hired gun seems to pre-sage the difficulties Wim would later encounter trying to work for Francis Ford Coppola on *Hammett*. Yet by placing all of this within the context of a "crime picture", Wenders is able to sidestep the indulgence of making a "struggling artist picture". It's not an entirely perfect marriage, but it sure makes for some interesting images, ideas and an amazing train sequence.

T2: Trainspotting

As much as I love Richard Linklater, his aesthetic hasn't really changed much over the years. Just think of *Boyhood* being shot over the course of twelve years and feeling like a cohesive whole. That's not the case with Danny Boyle.

Unlike the characters in *T2*, Boyle's famously hyperbolic style has evolved. Like the world around us, Danny's gone digital and has become much faster. The celluloid scenes from the original film that pop up from time to time stick out like sore thumbs among all the digital crispness - and that's the point. This movie is the equivalent of staying at a bar until closing time when all the lights come on and you see everything with crystal clarity. Every speck of dirt on the floor and wrinkle on your face is staring right back at you.

Close Encounters of the Third Kind

As much as I've enjoyed Steven Spielberg's recent output (especially *Catch Me If You Can*, *Munich* and *Tintin*) I feel like his most formally experimental films (and therefore most interesting to me) are *ET* and *Close Encounters*. Both films are about communication and in keeping with that theme, are more reliant on music and visual storytelling than dialogue to get their point across. It's not about narrative, it's about mood and feeling. Characters make decisions they cannot verbalize but we understand. The music and images do the speaking for them. The score and cinematography help to form a psychic connection between us and the characters. It's as though a message from the heavens has been planted inside of us. It's absolute cinematic alchemy.

Saving Private Ryan

From a narrative standpoint this movie didn't have to open with the D-Day Invasion. You could have easily snipped out those first twenty-six pages of screenplay, started with the telegrams being typed out, and gone from there. Sure there are little character beats that get dropped in that opening sequence (about Captain Miller in particular) but nothing that isn't also covered later. It feels like the type of indulgence that a studio reader would have suggested cutting for budget's sake. But this isn't a screenplay, this is a film. On the page it's a pretty straightforward account of taking the beach. But with sound and images on a screen, it's an assault. It beats you into the ground. That opening is there to traumatize the audience. Now you are in Captain Miller's boots. You're startled by loud noises and hypervigilant about threats from all sides. Is this what it's like to have PTSD? Anything can happen and anyone can die at any moment. And that is why Steven Spielberg is a master.

Guardians of the Galaxy, vol. 2

When the first *Guardians* film came out, I heard so many people rejoicing that Marvel had finally gotten "weird". And while I appreciated the humor, the soundtrack and some elements of the design, all I could think of was that Hunter S. Thompson quote, "It never got weird enough for me." Well lo and behold this sequel has come along to deliver on the promise of that first film.

Like Tim Burton did with *Batman Returns*, this is James Gunn bending the superhero genre towards himself. He played it safe for that first film, and now he's able to let his freak flag fly. This feels much more like the work of the mind that gave us *Tromeo & Juliet*, *Slither* and *Super*. Who other than Gunn would use a movie this expensive in order to dissect the insidious message of a 70's pop song?

No matter how fun and frivolous art can be, it's always telling us something. *Guardians of the Galaxy Vol. 2* is the perfect type of pop song: it's great to dance to, and the lyrics stick with you.

Kong: Skull Island

Lots of people take to criticizing filmmakers like Michael Bay and Zack Snyder for being "style without substance", but that's not really accurate. These films do have substance, it's just reprehensible substance that perpetuates a dangerous/delusional worldview. To demonize a prodigious use of imagery because of these guys is cinematic guilt by association. Thankfully, *Kong* came along to show us that there is another way.

Using the form of a Michael Bay film as well as Zack Snyder's preferred cinematographer, Jordan Vogt-Roberts is able to slyly subvert the Breitbart talking-points that usually accompany such spectacle, in favor of a more compassionate worldview. It isn't necessarily a "woke" film, but it is a wild popcorn flick that can be enjoyed without the guilt. The time has finally come for a baggage-less monster romp where someone dons a gas mask while wielding a samurai sword. Thank you, *Kong*.

Deep Red

When I think of Dario Argento films, I think of unbelievably thick latex. I remember all the kills in a particular film, but I remember them as these walled-off, insert shots where hatchets cut into foam-latex that is inches thick and only skin-colored on the outer layer. Divorced from the rest of the film it's rather comical. But when it's actually unfolding on screen, you find yourself imagining those things happening to your actual, non-latex skin. Within the context of the film, at 24 fps, it hurts. And that is why Dario Argento is a master. He can make you feel for a hunk of rubber like it was your own neck.

Yakuza Graveyard

I love the way that Kinji Fukasaku uses handheld. Lots of people do it his way nowadays (*The Wrestler*, *Narc*, *The Bourne Series*, etc.) but back then it was new. The only other filmmaker with a similar style was his American contemporary William Friedkin. It's not documentary and it's not French New Wave, it's something different. The camera is always in precisely the right place. It's never in danger of missing any crucial storytelling information. Yet, by virtue of the camera being handled, it's able to pull off all sorts of crazy shots to get an audience's adrenaline pumping. The camera swings wildly and can tilt or twirl at any moment. One could say that it's just as chaotic as the unpredictably violent world Fukasaku depicts in film after film. The perfect melding of style and substance.

Ornette: Made in America

While certainly flawed, this film comes closer than any other I've seen to an accurate cinematic representation of jazz. Shirley Clarke's editing has a great sense of rhythm that perfectly marries sound and vision. But she also understands the importance of solos. Sometimes the music gets to be front and center. Sometimes the visuals are allowed to take the lead. It's a delicate tapestry of new and old media that is filled to the brim with recurrent themes that are both aural and visual. Even the incorporation of video games seems to suggest the ways in which jazz assimilates new styles and techniques. As far as I know Shirley Clark didn't play an instrument, but through this film she pulls of a remarkable duet with one of American Music's most original voices ever.

Anomalisa

I love the way that Charlie Kaufman is able to craft endings. They aren't particularly showy and don't really rely on twists or reveals, but they really stick with you. Of course credit is due to the various directors who have helped him to realize these works, but it's no fluke that he is the unifying element there. While he might not like to talk about what his films "mean" the fact that we remember those endings serves as proof that there was something he wanted us to take from them. There was something he simply had to express. While certainly less image based than his work with Jonze and Gondry, *Anomalisa* is no different. It's a great Rorschach Test for how cynical of a person you are.

La La Land

I was sort of dreading this film. While I admire the craft of *Whiplash*, I found the overall message to be rather abhorrent. It was a self-justifying ode to being a dick. Knowing in advance that one of this film's main characters was a militant jazz evangelist, I was prepared for more of the same "ends justify the means" BS that college boys take way too to heart. Thankfully, this film allows its central dick to suffer (not a whole lot of suffering though, because in the end this is just light entertainment) but at least a little suffering. Rather than ending on the triumph of *Whiplash*, *La La Land* hangs around to see what comes after the success and does not shy away from the regret that follows. Was it really all worth it? Hopefully that's enough to prevent an army of militant jazz evangelists from springing up in this film's wake. It really is Emma Stone's movie anyway.

Greenberg

Thank God Noah Baumbach met Greta Gerwig! The misanthropy of *Margot at the Wedding* was almost too much to bear. Watching it I feared that Baumbach was already too far gone. I worried that it would become the blueprint for the rest of his career. And then he met Greta. Seeing as he was still with Jennifer Jason Leigh at the time, I know that there is no way Noah could have foresaw what Gerwig would mean for his future, but it's impossible to ignore the fact that in *Greenberg* she is playing the character who prompts a misanthrope to lighten up a little. And all his films since have been this perfect balance of cynicism and optimism. It's one hell of a streak. And it's all thanks to the ineffable charm of Greta Gerwig.

Blade Runner 2049

When this film was first announced I was very trepidatious. I'm very much not a Ridley Scott "Stan". While his technical skills are beyond reproach, it is often hard for me to find anything personal in his work. The original *Blade Runner* grew in my estimation when I discovered that it was made after the death of his brother Frank. He let his mourning creep into the work via the morose tone and slow pacing, and the film is better for it. Had he made that film at any other time in his life, that emotion would not have been there. It was a fluke. But how do you replicate a fluke? And how do you do that when the guy responsible for that fluke has been relegated to Executive Producer?

The blunt answer is that *Blade Runner 2049* did not manage to repeat that original's fluke - but that's OK. Instead of making me meditate on death, this film made me think about life. In *Blade Runner*, the Replicants want to live, simply to live. But what is the point of living when the world is so cold, the trees are dead and all the animals are synthetic. In *Blade Runner 2049* the Replicants have something to live for. Robin Wright's Lieutenant Joshi speaks about preserving a balance which is essentially an argument for stasis. *Blade Runner 2049* at least attempts to upend that stasis. Let's shake things up and see what happens. Tomorrow could be a brighter day.

The Grandmaster

The past plays a huge role in the work of Wong Kar Wai. His characters are haunted by friends, lovers and eras both long and recently departed. Wong's cinema recognizes that the passage of time is inevitable. Nothing can stop it. In this film in particular, characters are literally fighting the future via exquisitely staged kung fu battles. Yet, no matter who wins any particular match, history marches on. It is a wave that cannot be stopped. Some things are allowed to endure. Others are pulled out to sea in a rip current. Those are the cold, hard facts. Yet unlike other Wong Kar Wai films which tend to focus on the person in mourning, this film gives voice to the one being mourned as well. Nobody gets an easy break.

Meadowland

Generally, beauty and quality are considered to be mutually exclusive. If someone or something is beautiful, they/it must not be significant. A beautiful actress simply cannot be anything but a pretty face to sell tickets, and cinematographers who turn to directing can only make gorgeous films that lack thematic depth. Right? *Meadowland* roundly refutes both of those assertions. Cinematographer Reed Morano's feature debut consistently puts emotion before aesthetics and the whole thing is anchored by an uncompromisingly honest performance from the amazing Olivia Wilde. The beauty is just icing on the cake.

The Ladies Man

While Jerry Lewis certainly wears his influences on his sleeve (Tashlin and Tati) there's no denying that he also had an instinctual eye for images. Though the "plot" consists of little more than a series of vaguely connected vignettes, the imagery and jokes are enough to hold your attention. Jerry Lewis is what Adam Sandler could become if he actually gave a damn. The size of that set and the precision of he choreography is enough to give *Rear Window* a run for its money, and it's all in service of getting the laugh. Jerry was not content to just clown around. He took his silliness seriously and it shows. We really did lose a legend.

The Intern

I've heard it said that one of the problems with becoming a successful artist is that once you are successful you're no longer in touch with the average Joe or Jane. You are able to afford things that they cannot. Your problems are not their problems. Many people like to level this criticism at Nancy Meyers. They accuse her of making films exclusively for upper middle-class WASPs who have well-appointed kitchens. It's a fair criticism, but it also shouldn't negate any of her work's various other virtues. I was absolutely taken with how warm-hearted this film is. Everyone is so damn nice. There are no bad guys, the stakes are extremely low and everyone is well intentioned. It certainly isn't great cinema, but it sure does make for a pleasant way to spend two hours. I had a smile on my face from start to finish and that's a good thing.

Love & Friendship

If I had to sum up acting and directing in a single word, that word would be "nuance." Words on a page can be delivered in so many different ways. This is why high school kids hate Shakespeare. Read alone for homework, Romeo and Juliet can be pretty dry stuff. With the right actors and directors it can become a laugh riot. The same goes for the work of Jane Austen. Throughout *Love & Friendship* I found myself imagining a David Mamet version of this same story with actors merely reciting the script and giving zero inflection. Thankfully, Whit Stillman and his actors chose to wring every possible drop of comedy out of this material. I predict this film will fast become a favorite for substitute teachers to show English classes.

Detective Story

Theatre and Film share so much in common, yet in very crucial ways they're worlds apart. They both use actors, sets, costumes and lighting. They both rely on scripts and are viewed by theaters full of people. But translating a good play to the screen is actually rather challenging. Often the finished film will betray its origins as a play through its limited number of locations. You feel like there is no real world outside the set where this story is taking place. That's certainly not the case with this William Wyler adaptation. This film is alive! People come in and out, this character interacts with that character, etc. It feels like a real police precinct where we are but a fly on the wall. And like a real fly, we get to move all over the place and see everything from the best angles. People who say Wyler was a lesser director can go take a long walk off a short pier.

Captain America: Civil War

The other day on Twitter, critic Scott Weinberg asked for people's opinion of "...the #1 BEST feature film based on a Marvel superhero". I replied, "*Iron Man 3* because it's about consequences and is amplified by Downey's personal history. Also it has an auteur's stamp." While the Russo Brothers are far too early in their collective career to have a discernible "stamp", they sure as hell understand consequences and how to wring every possible emotion out of them. It makes sense that they began in television where it's all about the actions of one week having ramifications in the next. Lots of people are saying that TV is becoming more and more like film, but the door swings the other way as well. I can certainly foresee a day where this interconnectivity becomes impenetrable and annoying, but right now we are in an amazingly sweet spot and I can't wait to see where it goes next. Also, Robert Downey Jr.'s checkered past helps a lot.

The Disaster Artist

Much like James Franco, this film wants to be taken seriously. It's about a silly movie and centered around a silly (real life) character, but it wants to treat it all seriously. *The Disaster Artist* wants to be about friendship, relationships, art, insanity, etc. This is what Tommy was striving for too. If you ask him what *The Room* is about, he will tell you that it is about everything.

While Franco's endeavor was much more successful than Tommy's, it is also similarly hamstrung by its ambition. It's about so many things that it ends up being about very little. It has thoughts and ideas and things to say, but they don't add up to anything too profound. They are all truisms that we have heard before. I know Franco has a mind for Meta, but I don't think even he was aware of this subtextual level. Like Tommy, he just stumbled into success.

Heat

While I certainly don't agree with Pauline Kael's opinion that the Auteur Theory was a way for film-bros to label the genre films of their youths as "art", *Heat* certainly gives me similar feelings. As much as I enjoy this film, there's nothing deep about it. It has nothing new to say about cops and criminals, and the "insights" it has about men and women are equally reductive. But that doesn't stop people from trying to read more into it. Why do people feel the need to graft deep thoughts onto this film? Does a work really need to be filled with soul-shattering insight in order to be great? Can't an expertly crafted piece of Pop Cinema just be enough? The photography, choreography, editing, score, sound, and acting are all top notch. It's a whole crew of absolute professionals doing their absolute best and it's a wonder to behold. Can't that just be enough?

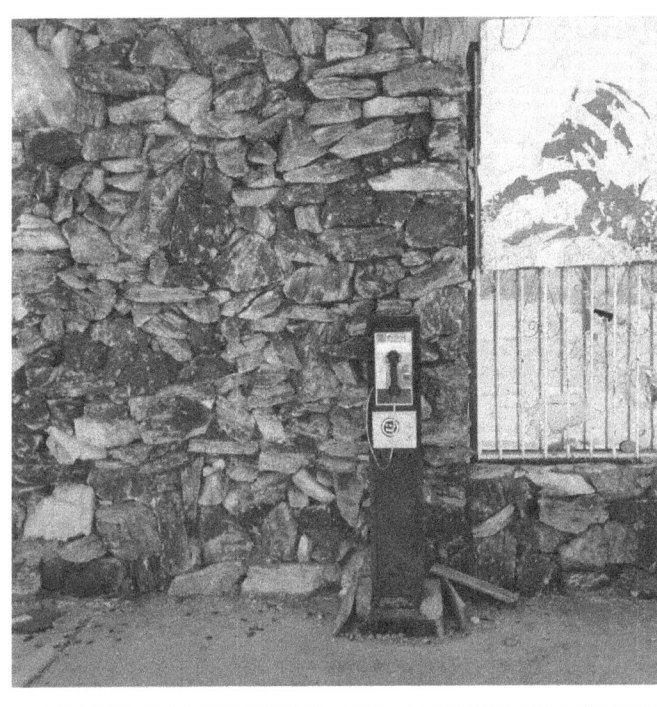

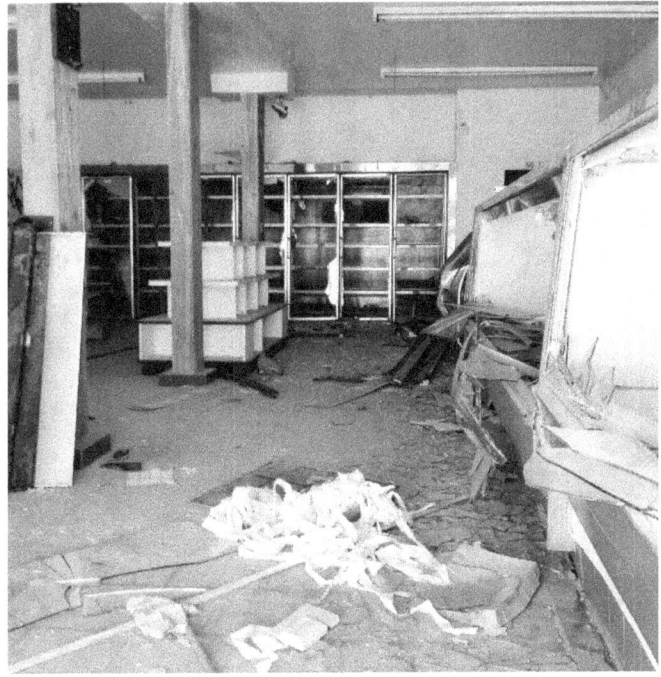

Playlist No. 42

-It's Like That/Run-DMC

-San Antonio Rose/Patsy Cline

-The Long Way Home/Norah Jones

-Ol' 55/Tom Waits

-Only the Good Die Yound/Billy Joel

-The More You Ignore Me (The Closer I Get)/Morrissey

-La Nevada (Theme)/Gil Evans

-Jungle Love/Morris Day & the Time

-Tricherahops/Too Many Zooz

-Teenage Dream/Katy Perry

-Unbelievers/Vampire Weekend

-Alright/Kendrick Lamar

The World

The Decline of Western Civilization

While it might seem weird to say in this era of everyone having a camera on them at all times: This film really reinforces the importance of documenting your scene. If you aren't doing it, who is? The Germs only have one full-length album and frontman Darby Crash was already dead by the time this film was released. But thanks to Penelope Spheeris' camera, he can live on for forever. I know we are all supposed to put our phones down and actually experience life, but if you really think something is awesome and worth sharing, please record it and share it. The world needs more awesome things. Don't be so selfish. Spread the wealth. You might be preserving something which would have otherwise been forgotten.

Real Life

I think this film would make a great double-bill with David Bryne's *True Stories,* as both films are actively focused on exposing just how surreal "reality" can actually be. When viewed through the right lens, anything can be abnormal or weird. To Charles Grodin's Dr. Yeager, surgery on a horse is par for the course (of course) but to us it is an inspired bit of comic absurdism. By placing this faux-documentary construct on the film we are able to appreciate just how oblivious people can be of their own situations. Just look at how the fictionalized, "neutral" Albert Brooks character is incapable of stepping outside of himself enough to see just how weird it is to begin this grand experiment with a musical number and orchestra. And so, even though the "experiment" is a "failure", it's actually a success. This is how people behave. This is Real Life.

In the Cut

If I were a filmmaker, I would not want to get anywhere near this material. Due to my privilege as a straight, cis-gender male, I've never had to constantly fear for my safety the way a female, homosexual, or trans person does. I don't have to worry about roughly half of the world's population potentially wishing me harm. The threat of physical and sexual violence is completely alien to me. Yet, as an audience member I find this topic to be extremely compelling. Through Jane Campion and Meg Ryan I am able to glimpse that experience from the comfort and safety of my own sofa. Only a female, trans, or queer filmmaker could have told this story. Imagine some straight, male director talking about how the danger of everyday life can sometimes be a turn on. No way! What danger do they know? Although, a male person of color does know the unique terror of living in a world where black lives don't seem to matter. You know, the more I think about it, this story isn't very niche at all. The only group this is a foreign idea to is the tiny minority group of straight, white, cis-gender males. And that is the power of cinema.

The Invitation

Is grief the cinematic inverse of disaster? Since 9/11 both of these themes have become fertile ground for cinema. On one end you have films like *Man of Steel* and *Star Trek Into Darkness* which traffic in the iconography of that fateful day without speaking much to the underlying causes and/or aftermath. On the other end you have films like this, *The Babadook* and *Rabbit Hole* which dwell in the unending pain and uncertainty which follows such a catastrophic loss. Neither type of film really supplies any answers. But at least the grief films feel more honest. Few of these films get more honest than the very final reveal of this film. It's pretty powerful stuff.

The Witness

How much of a news story do you have to read to be outraged? How much of a news story do you have to read before you click that "share" button on Facebook? While I'm sure plenty of you share responsibly, I know for a fact that plenty also share stories based entirely on the headline. I do it myself. And that's how false information spreads. This film is not a click-bait headline. This film is a "long read". This film goes deep and goes wide. You think you know the story of Kitty Genovese, but even her own family didn't know her whole story. Can anyone really know the whole story? Does the quest ever end?

Jackie

Say what you will about Natalie Portman's performance (which I personally adore) but there is no way to deny that this film is a subjective masterpiece. It literally puts you in the high-heeled shoes of Jackie Kennedy. Pablo Larrain and his collaborators make you realize that though she came from money and became First Lady, as a woman, a wife, and a public figure, Jackie had almost no agency. Everyone has an opinion on what she should should do or say. Every action is second guessed. And then her husband's head blows up. Suddenly, all bets are off. In the chaotic days after JFK's assassination, Jackie sees a chance to take control for once and she seizes it with both hands. She is a woman liberated and that is a beautiful thing to behold.

Mudbound

My favorite niche, sub-genre is Movies About America. I'm a total sucker for stories that are subtextually about our Nation as a whole. *Citizen Kane, The Godfather* series, and *There Will Be Blood* spring most readily to mind, but greed isn't America's only defining trait. There's also the small matter of white people enslaving black people for hundreds of years.

It's no accident that this film opens with two white guys digging a grave for their racist father and finding the skull of a murdered slave. Slavery is literally just under the surface of this film and it informs every interaction between the numerous characters in this ensemble. The story might be set in the 1940's, but much of this film looks like the 1840's because The South is literally stuck in the past. Since the Civil War we have been trying to move forward without addressing slavery and Jim Crow. We are mudbound and will continue to be so until we take a long, hard look in the mirror. A film set 70 years in the past shouldn't be so relevant, but here we are.

Get Out

Jordan Peele's *Get Out* is really an embarrassment of riches. There is so much to talk about. Both the filmmaking itself and the social issues covered in this film are equally fertile grounds for discussion and dissection. Though there are many intensely specific conversations one can have about this film, the one that grabbed me the most was the choice of victims.

The Armitage Family aren't just picking generic black people to foist themselves into, they are picking black people with potential. Though we don't know it at first, we later discover that the opening victim was a budding jazz musician, Chris is clearly shown to be an up and coming photographer, and near the end we see Rose looking for promising student athletes. All I could think about was names like Trayvon Martin, Michael Brown and Tamir Rice: young men taken from this earth before they had a chance to make their mark.

And what are these white people doing with that potential? Are they taking the glory for themselves? Worse, they are squandering those gifts. A once promising jazz musician is reduced to being some white woman's meek, arm candy. A once promising athlete is reduced to splitting logs. And a promising photographer is about to become some old, art dealer's new eyes. All of that promise squandered by rich people who already had their bite at the apple and want more. And that is the real horror in this film.

Black Girl

Straight and to the point. This is European colonialism in a microcosm. If the ending takes you by surprise, you weren't paying attention. It's not overt racism that does the real damage to someone's self-worth. It's indifference and self-interest that hold an entire People back from their true potential. Racial slurs and physical violence are certainly abhorrent and hurtful, but a lifetime filled with people taking advantage of you simply because of your situation, combined with others who are either indifferent to that situation or who do only the bare minimum, is what can really destroy a soul.

13th

There is no room for ambiguity in this documentary. Ava DuVernay has a message to impart and she wants to make damn sure that you get it. While she never resorts to Michael Moore narration or Errol Morris recreations, the bravura editing by Spencer Averick (obviously under DuVernay's direction) makes damn sure that nothing is lost on anyone. A single cut can bridge 150 years and help us to better understand how we got into this mess in the first place. Sure it's unsubtle, that's deliberate. DuVernay knows how important it is to pick the right tool for the job. If you want to carve the statue of David, you use a chisel. If you want to tear down the Prison Industrial Complex, you use a sledge hammer. I'm glad that this film is on Netflix so that it can be seen by as many people as possible because this is a documentary for right now.

O.J.: Made in America

Back in 2000 there was a TV movie about the OJ case titled *American Tragedy*. I remember at the time thinking that the title was quite an overstatement for a film about an ex-athlete's murder trial. It's not like Simpson was a politician or something. Someday I'll check that movie out, but having now consumed over seven hours of expertly crafted documentary filmmaking on the subject, I completely agree with that title.

It's twenty years later and all of the issues at play during the first trial are still problems today. Rather than showing us how far we have come in two decades, this film makes us acutely aware that nothing has changed. In fact, things have gotten worse. This is not a nostalgia piece. This film is relevant to the here and now. Orenthal James Simpson might have fallen from a great height, but it's nothing compared to how far American Culture has fallen. If Spike Lee had made this film, it would have ended or began with someone yelling, "WAKE UP!"

I am Not Your Negro

It's insane that a piece conceived decades ago is still relevant today. It's what happens when you choose to ignore a problem rather than confront it. You call something a "riot" rather than an "uprising" or "protest" so that you can diminish it and write it off. When you treat a tragedy as a one-off, rather than a symptom of something greater, you diminish our ability to get at the heart of the disease. Bury your head in the sand all you want, but there is something gravely wrong with this country and the issue of race. Having a black President for eight years allowed us to further the delusion, and look where that got us! The information in this film is not new. We just need to finally accept what it is saying and look within ourselves. Otherwise, what hope is there for a brighter tomorrow?

Philadelphia

I wish I had seen this film when it first came out. As the son of a huge Bruce Springsteen fan I was certainly aware of it, but I didn't actually seek out and watch it until five or so years ago. And while both viewings moved me greatly, I also felt like I was watching AIDS, homophobia and bigotry 101. I was watching this film in an After Ellen world where HIV/AIDS is still incurable, but it is also no longer a death sentence. It's amazing how fast the world can change.

It's also amazing that it took thirteen years for Hollywood to address this plague. I get that the GOP was ignoring it because they were fine with it killing off gay men and IV drug users, but homosexuals have formed the bedrock of the entertainment industry since forever. Why did it take active protesting of the Oscars and of hit films like *Silence of the Lambs* and *Basic Instinct* to get the Coastal Elites on board?

Philadelphia remains an important film worth watching for its strong performances and Demme's compassionate direction, but more so than anything it is a reminder of how slow to action even the most progressive people can be when there isn't someone actively pushing them to do right. If you want to get something done, you can't be silent.

Brazil

Early in their friendship, Peter Bogdanovich confided to Orson Welles that he wasn't too fond of the legendary auteur's adaptation of Franz Kafka's *The Trial*. Years later, Orson informed Peter that he had intended the film to be a comedy. Viewed in this light, Bogdanovich was much better able to appreciate the pitch black comedy at the heart of Welles' bureaucratic nightmare. No added context is needed in order to appreciate *Brazil*. The comedy is right there at the surface. How can you not find humor in all the paperwork and Rube Goldberg technology? It's all so wild and whimsical that the horror is able to really creep up on you. True evil doesn't come at you with a bunch of gloom and doom. True evil comes at you with a smile that looks as jolly and well-meaning as Michael Palin's.

Zama

Calling a film about colonialism, "surreal" is redundant. It's the forced collision of two disparate worlds, how can it not yield odd or unexpected juxtapositions? Of course the culture of the colonizer dominates, but it is impossible for the colonized to be completely assimilated. Spain is not The Borg. A colony is neither fish nor fowl, it is a completely new entity. This is the world of Zama. A world where men and women wear wigs despite the tropical climate, and slaves in loincloths also wear jackets as they deliver important pronouncements. It's a film that really creeps up on you, like Jim Jarmusch's *Dead Man*. The final act is worth the price of admission alone.

Lost in America

Just as this generation is overrun with movies about Millennials needing to get their lives together, the 1980's was packed to the gills with movies about Yuppies in crisis. While not strictly following the model of films like *After Hours* and *Something Wild, Lost in America* really does fit the bill. But instead of being beset by a number of outside forces symbolizing problems in their lives, David and Linda are out to destroy David and Linda. They are 100% responsible for everything that happens to them. There's no big bad guy to vanquish. They are the big bad guy. And in perfect bad guy fashion, their crisis is solved with the help of white, cishet privilege. They are pathetic characters and we laugh at them, but how much are we actually laughing at ourselves?

The Marriage of Maria Braun

For better or worse, when you make a period piece you are judging the past. Often the judgement is positive. Weren't things so much better back in the day? This rose colored perspective almost always ignores the various horrors that were going on during the time period in question. As a German man born almost immediately after the end of World War II, Rainer Werner Fassbinder has nothing good to say about the past. Using Maria Braun as a stand-in for the entire country, Fassbinder paints a very bleak portrait of post-war Germany. Not only is Maria an opportunist who will do anything to move forward financially, she also continues to carry a torch for her missing/imprisoned Nazi husband. An entire Nation doesn't just suddenly change their prejudices or impulses overnight and the "progress" of today is often built on a rotten foundation. We are forever wedded to the past. Fassbinder never wants us to forget that.

Mildred Pierce

Veda is the perfect scapegoat. Remove her from this film and you have the story of a woman who is destroyed by her ambitious quest for the American Dream that we are all told to want. With her, you have the story of this poor woman whose only sin was that she cares too much. Did James M. Cain intend for her to be a cipher? She's this perfect void that will never be filled no matter how much love or money you throw at it. She's both voracious and insatiable. Just when you think you've got it all with your chain of restaurants and nice house, along comes Veda to throw a new wrench into the perfectly running machinery. It's a series of false peaks that leads only to destruction. But I didn't do it for me. I did it for her! There is no happy end. When you fall down a bottomless pit, you die of starvation.

The Manchurian Candidate

Prior to World War II, America was A world power. After World War II, we were THE world power. Unlike Japan and all the various countries of Europe, there was no rebuilding necessary. It was much easier for us to get back to (more or less) business as usual. Suddenly we were top dog. So of course we suddenly became very preoccupied with maintaining this new status. Some might even call it paranoia. But can you really blame us? The Great Depression was still very prominent in our National Rearview. People could remember what it was like to be hungry. Trauma like that sticks with you. You might not be aware of it, but it's there. It's in the back of your mind waiting to be triggered. And so, practically overnight, New Deal Democrats like Frank Sinatra, Ronald Reagan, Charlton Heston and a significant portion of America were primed to be activated by the Republican Party's message of blatant self-interest. So what if two Kennedys and a King had to die? They sure as hell were not going to go hungry again.

A Face in the Crowd

Thanks to the rise of Donald Trump, this film is on the minds of a lot of people. Lately I've heard a lot of people claiming that it's time to add *A Face in the Crowd* to the continually growing list of films that were once considered satires, but are now defacto documentaries. But as 'Becca'lise pointed out to me after our most recent viewing, regardless of how dark this film is, it is actually pretty optimistic. I'm not sure if Lonesome Rhodes' downfall was mandated by the production code or what, but the idea that a demagogue like that could be brought down by a few offhand remarks is actually wishful thinking. As we have seen over and over again with "The Donald", shocking statements are not enough in today's America. People decry our "Outrage Culture" and the ways that it can destroy lives over trivial faux pas, but it has somehow yet to put an end to that man's candidacy. In fact, those outrageous statements have only made him stronger. Perhaps we should instead move this from the "satire" column to the "fantasy" column?

Weiner

The fact that this documentary exists is insane. But it's also kind of the point. This is a portrait of a man so drunk on power that he believes he can get away with anything. This is a portrait of a man who cannot tell when it's over. So of course he allowed cameras to keep filming his zombie campaign. I get the impulse to counter the mainstream media story by allowing people to see "the real Anthony Weiner", but how can you be so blind as to not realize the way you are coming off in all this candid footage? I don't even know if Donald Trump has that much ego! As head-shaking and vomit inducing as this whole mess is on a personal and political level, it sure does make for riveting and fascinating cinema. Oh and if you're reading this on the day that it posts, please go out and vote tomorrow.

Nocturama

No matter what, violence is inherently cinematic. Filmmakers can make it horrific and traumatizing or they can make it ludicrous and comical, but the sheer kineticism of such acts cannot help but catch our eye. It goes right to that, "lizard brain" we hear so much about, and connects with us on a primal level. It's the same sort of psychology that you hear about advertisers employing to make us want their their products. Do you think that ISIS and the Alt-Right have teleconferences to discuss branding? Somebody has to give the social media guy a set of guidelines to follow, right?

Viva

With its leisurely pace, it's impossible to miss how much work went into this film. To match the specific look Anna Biller and her collaborators were going for, all these period props and costumes had to be found or made. The same goes for the sets and locations. The result is gorgeous to look at and filled with bare flesh, but thanks to the presentational acting and blatant sloganeering, it's much closer to Jean-Luc Godard than Russ Meyer. Biller wants us to take something away from this film. Like Guy Maddin, she's using the form of vintage media to deconstruct the artificiality of both the past and the present. You become hyper-aware of the sexism and hypocrisy that was just underneath the surface of the "free love" movement and America in general. With a Trump presidency looming, a film like *Viva* provides as an uneasy reminder of the "good times" red hats want to get back to.

Married to the Mob

The instant we meet Angela de Marco we know that she doesn't fit in this world. She looks the part of a mob wife with her big hair and hoop earrings, but there is a look in her eyes that tells us she wants more. She is distracted. She is somewhere else. She isn't like all the other catty broads in this beauty salon.

There were a lot of movies like this in the 80's, about trying to break out of the conformity. Usually it's a story about leaving behind square, yuppie suburbia for something more exciting. Jonathan Demme even made one of these films two years prior with the masterful *Something Wild*. But what makes this film stand out from the pack is the decision to substitute Reagan's America with the world of organized crime. It makes Angela's urge to flee a bit more understandable to the average viewer. It also makes a nice parallel between the Reagan Administration and gangsters. Bonus points for having a female protagonist. It's sort of odd that this is the film that preceded *The Silence of the Lambs*, but it also makes sense.

A League of their Own

Pretty sure this was my first viewing in at least twenty years. The danger with such big gaps is that sometimes the film that is actually in front of you doesn't live up to the memory. Luckily for me, I remembered very little of this film. I remembered stuff like "No crying in baseball" and some of the Rosie O'Donnell goofing around (because that's the kind of stuff that appeals to a prepubescent boy who hasn't yet turned into a horn-dog) but much of the rest felt brand new to me. What I was really taken by was the extremely minimal plot. Essentially this is a hang-out movie. The film is enjoyable because we enjoy these characters and like spending time with them. It's also a great look at the gulf between image and reality. By contrasting how these women actually lived and behaved with the staged photos and newsreels that went out to the world, Penny Marshall and her collaborators are subtly chipping away at the conservative idealization of the past. It's not a film with a radical, feminist agenda, but it does have something to say, and it says it well.

Toni Erdmann

On paper this sounds like a film that would fill multiplexes. It also sounds like something we've seen a million times before: Joker parent needs to learn that not everything is a joke, serious child needs to loosen up, and everyone learns and grows. As I was watching it, I kept imagining these same scenes being played out with bright lighting and crisp lines and the mere thought made me cringe. It's the makings of an Adam Sandler for Netflix film. Fortunately this movie is not shot that way.

Director Maren Ade's choice to place this generically farcical story in a very believable world helps to expose just how generic and farcical our world actually is. Especially the world of business! If you are hoping to climb the corporate ladder, there's practically no end to the ways in which you will debase yourself for advancement. You'll also let a whole lot slide in order to not be seen as difficult. Go along to get along. The world of this film is not a fiction. We are living in it. Donald Trump is President.

Born in Flames

It's depressing how prescient this film turned out to be - and I'm not even talking about that last sequence. The idea of a utopia in name only that came about because of a peaceful revolution feels a lot like the eight years of

Obama that we just lived through. We were able to pretend that everything had changed overnight without all the messy business of addressing the racism, xenophobia, misogyny and homophobia that eventually made Trump possible. The future depicted in this film even had a Black President!

When we were watching this the other night 'Becca'lise proclaimed, "This feels like a zine!" and I don't think I could have said it any better. I was already thinking about how this felt like mid-60's Godard (when he was stating to get political but had not yet lost his sense of fun) but my wife's observation is really more apt. This film owes way more to punk and queer culture than it does to Bertolt Brecht and Nicholas Ray. Moreso than cinema, this is reportage. Dispatches from the future. Now, if only we'd really listened to Lizzie and the girls all those years ago. Anyone have a time machine?

The Hateful Eight

1/1/16

I went into *The Hateful Eight* with a lot of expectations. It was the Tarantino film that almost wasn't (because the script had been leaked) and it was shot on Ultra Panavision 70. I came out of it very nonplussed.

Though it was shot with large format film and lenses, nearly the entire runtime was spent inside a not particularly cinematic cabin. And then there was also the question of misogyny. While I'm aware that Tarantino has written some seriously awesome female characters in the past, I absolutely could not figure out what he was trying to say here. Needless to say I wasn't really chomping at the bit to revisit this film any time soon.

It's nearly eighteen months later and I decide to give it another try. And while the Cinema of this filmed stage play still leaves much to be desired, I got a lot more out of it this time. I'm still not certain what Quentin was trying to do with this picture, but having lived through the 2016 Election and five months of Trump, the world of this film is now a much more recognizable one. It's not a straight analogy where A = X or anything like that, but this duplicitous world where everyone has a hidden agenda and rivals miraculously become unlikely allies, feels just like turning on the evening news. And of course it's particularly bad for the women. God bless America!

Star Wars: Episode VIII – The Last Jedi

I know this movie was conceived and shot before the 2016 Election, but it really feels like a film for right this instant. When watching it the first time, the stream of setbacks that befall The Resistance felt structurally off. But when contrasted with The Trump Era where Healthcare, Civil Rights, Women's Rights, LGBTQ Rights, etc. are all under continuous and simultaneous attack - the pace felt kind of leisurely. Having this come out the same week as Doug Jones' victory in Alabama seems almost too perfect. Too bad the title *A New Hope* was already taken. Or maybe they're preparing us for the gut-punch at the start of *Episode IX* where the First Order gives a tax cut to all the arms manufacturers on Canto Bight.

Shin Godzilla

A film does not have to be grim and gritty to be grounded and realistic. This reboot is miles away from the insanity of something like *Invasion of Astro-Monster*, while also not falling under the 'blink and you missed it' approach of Gareth Edwards' *Godzilla.* Like the original 1954 *Gojira,* this is a film about Japan right now with images that recall Fukushima and the earthquake that preceded it. This is a film about how we handle a disaster. It's about a group of people trying to do the right thing in a completely uncharted situation. There is no bad guy. Everyone is just doing their best. Yes they make some big miscalculations, but this is a situation that nobody could have prepared for. Not even the giant lizard destroying Tokyo is really bad. He's just doing his giant lizard thing. In a world that's so full of darkness, it's nice to see something...hopeful?

Step

As Roger Ebert famously stated, "Movies are the most powerful empathy machine in all the arts." When I watch movies from foreign countries like Iran, I often think about how beneficial it would be for all Americans to watch them. They would be shocked at how much they share in common with people a world away who are supposedly our, "enemy". The same could be said about a documentary like *Step.* It's sad to think that it would require a film to make people realize how much they have in common with someone they share a country with, but that's the world we live in today. There are so many outlets for information and entertainment that people are able to live in a carefully curated bubble just for them where they only see/hear things that reinforce what they already believe. That's why art like this documentary is important. It bursts the bubble and helps us recognize our shared humanity.

Wonder Woman

Oh man this movie is everything I love about Super Hero Comics: it's silly, serious, action-packed, and it has an ethos. I 100% reject the idea of keeping politics and social issues out of genre, and so does this film. It has a message to impart and it imparts it while also telling a pulpy, "blood and thunder" story that's filled with gods, goddesses, and super-powered Germans. More than ever we need super heroes, but since they don't exist, we have to become them. Wonder Woman herself cannot come down off the screen and save us, but she can inspire a whole generation of little girls and boys to care for others and to fight for what they believe in. Now, let's cue up that electric strings sting, and get to work.

Black Panther

While other films in the Marvel Cinematic Universe have dealt with issues of treaties and succession, I would never consider them to be political films. Though the *Guardians of the Galaxy* films make it more apparent than some of the others, in the end they're all about family dynamics. Even Captain America and Iron Man's conflict is little more than a heightened version of most dinner tables at The Holidays.

When MCU movies are topical it is either in a vague sense (ie: platitudes about sticking up for the little guy) or simply by refuting the carnage of DC's cinematic output. *Black Panther*, on the other hand, is very specifically topical and political. It talks specifically about refugees and barriers that keep people out. It also talks about disadvantaged communities and how helping them is more involved than just saving the planet from annihilation every other week. And of course there is the fact that this cast is predominantly black and overwhelmingly female in the era of #BlackLivesMatter and #MeToo.

The fact that there was a concerted effort to diminish this film by lowering its rating on Rotten Tomatoes or claiming that white attendees were subjected to physical violence at screenings, let's you know that the "other side" was aware of this film's power. And the fact that this film smashed so many records let's you know that audiences the world over are thirsty for what it is selling.

This is not a one-off. This is a repeatable model. Hire non-white actors and crews. Hire and cast women. People are sick of having to identify with a token either in front of or behind the camera. May the one-two punch of *Wonder Woman* and *Black Panther* be the blast that finally opens the floodgates!

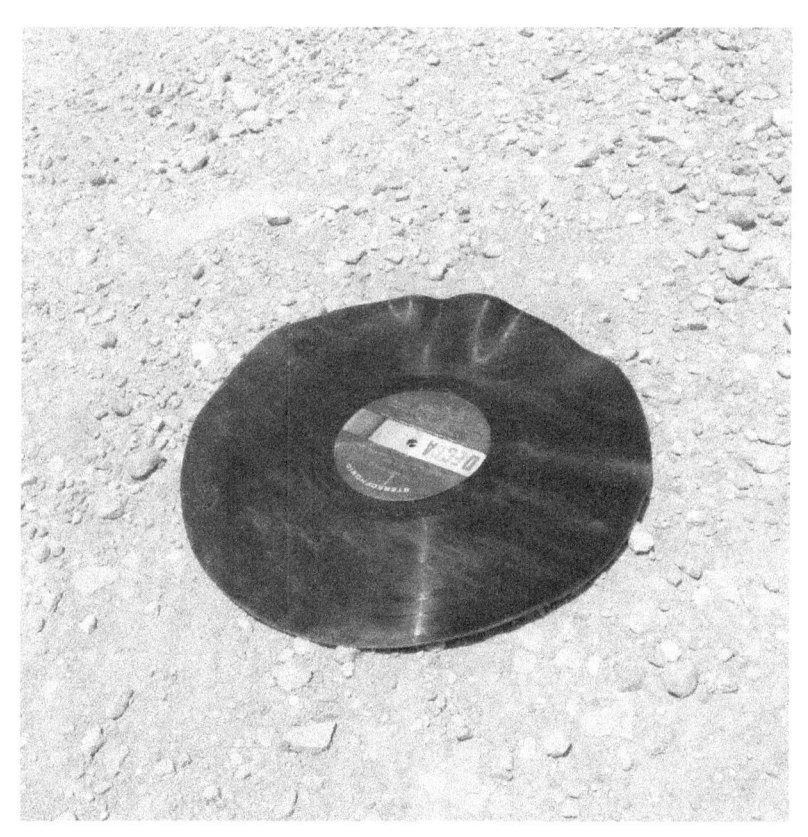

Playlist No. 44

-If I Knew You Were Comin' I'd've Baked a Cake/Eileen Barton with the New Yorkers

-Australia/The Shins

-Dream Lover/The Paris Sisters

-Girlfriend in a Coma/The Smiths

-I'm a Cuckoo (Avalanches Remix)/Belle and Sebastian

-Changing Partners/Helen Forrest

-No Other Love/Jo Stafford

-Smoke Gets in Your Eyes/The Platters

-Royals/Puddles Pitty Party

-Angel Baby/Rosie & the Originals

-My Little Corner of the World/Yo La Tengo

-The Promise/When in Rome

Junkies

The world of film financing these days is the Wild West and you have to take whatever opportunities come your way, lest you miss out on a chance to tell your story. But what seemed prudent last year could come back to bite you in the end. Did Martin Scorsese know he was helping to launder stolen Malaysian Money when he agreed to direct *The Wolf of Wall Street*? Probably not, but that's what happened. And due diligence will only shield you so far.

Remember when a movie from Warner Brothers had only one logo at the front of the film? Now it feels like you're attending an animation festival with the un-ending stream of production logos preceding a feature. Are you sure you know where all these Executive Producers got their millions from? Getting caught up with unscrupulous financiers used to be the burden of indie filmmakers like the one depicted in Alexandre Rockwell's *In the Soup*. But nowadays, you have "studio" films like *Wonder Woman* receiving funds from the likes of Brett Ratner! And of course there's all that Chinese Money we keep hearing about. Everybody's hustling. Just check out the documentary *Seduced and Abandoned*, directed by...Oh...

When you step back and really look at the big picture, you understand why someone like Steven Soderbergh would want to abandon the Film World for the solitude of painting. The idea of needing nothing other than paint and a canvas to express yourself must be very tempting. Yet since, "retiring" Soderbergh has directed two features, a TV series, and an interactive app. I guess Frank Capra was right when he said:

"Film is a disease. When it infects your bloodstream, it takes over as the number one hormone. It bosses the enzymes, directs the pineal gland, plays Iago to your psyche. As with heroin, the antidote to film is more film."

Anything for a fix, right? And we who watch and write are not innocent, either. I believe the term is Co-Dependent?

Personal Pantheon

On my 31st Birthday, 'Becca'lise suggested I commemorate the occasion by posting a list of my 31 favorite films on the blog. I continued the tradition with 32 more films on my 32nd birthday, and 33 films on my 33rd birthday. I did 34 for my 34th but didn't publish it to the blog.

What follows is a list of my personal 130 Favorite films. I limited myself to one film per director on each go-around to prevent it from becoming just a bunch of full filmographies.

- *Pulp Fiction*
- *Ed Wood*
- *Dr. Strangelove*
- *Taxi Driver*
- *L.A. Confidential*
- *Y Tu Mamá También*
- *Buffalo '66*
- *The Godfather Part II*
- *Annie Hall*
- *Boogie Nights*
- *Chasing Amy*
- *The Blues Brothers*
- *Vertigo*
- *Singin' in the Rain*
- *Ghostbusters*
- *The Graduate*
- *Blue Velvet*
- *The Third Man*
- *Nashville*

- *Rushmore*
- *8 ½*
- *JFK*
- *The Big Lebowski*
- *Being John Malkovich*
- *High and Low*
- *Alphaville*
- *Some like it hot*
- *Talk to Her*
- *Harold and Maude*
- *Female Trouble*
- *A Night at the Opera*
- *Il Sorpasso*
- *Twin Peaks: Fire Walk with Me*
- *Young Frankenstein*
- *The Departed*
- *Yoyo*
- *A Clockwork Orange*

- *Rosemary's Baby*
- *The Black Cat*
- *Red Desert*
- *King of Kong: A Fistful of Quarters*
- *Dead Ringers*
- *The Right Stuff*
- *E.T. The Extraterrestrial*
- *A Serious Man*
- *Zero Dark Thirty*
- *There Will Be Blood*
- *Do the Right Thing*
- *Hannah and Her Sisters*
- *Something Wild (1986)*
- *Blow Out*
- *Kill Bill vol. 1 & 2*
- *Apocalypse Now*
- *Z*
- *To Be or Not to Be (1942)*
- *The Red Shoes*
- *The Long Goodbye*
- *Pan's Labyrinth*
- *The Iron Giant*
- *Scott Pilgrim vs. the World*
- *Zodiac*
- *The Exorcist*
- *Rear Window*
- *State of Siege*
- *McCabe & Mrs. Miller*
- *North by Northwest*
- *Lady Snowblood*
- *Black Swan*
- *Beginners*
- *Gilda*
- *Possession (1981)*
- *Little Shop of Horrors*

- *Los Angeles Plays Itself*
- *Shaun of the Dead*
- *Inherent Vice*
- *Frances Ha*
- *The Royal Tenenbaums*
- *The Rules of the Game*
- *On the Waterfront*
- *Jackie Brown*
- *Persepolis*
- *Aguirre, the Wrath of God*
- *Goodfellas*
- *2001: A Space Odyssey*
- *Journey to Italy*
- *Arabian Nights (1974)*
- *The Umbrellas of Cherbourg*
- *Citizen Kane*
- *Sleeping Beauty (1959)*
- *Fargo*
- *Fox and His Friends*
- *La Dolce Vita*
- *Charade*
- *Morvern Callar*
- *The Last Days of Disco*
- *Invasion of the Body Snatchers (1978)*
- *Mildred Pierce (1945)*
- *His Girl Friday*
- *Crash (1996)*
- *Carol*
- *The Social Network*
- *The Silence of the Lambs*
- *Capote*
- *Eyes Wide Shut*
- *Mad Max: Fury Road*

- *Margaret*
- *The Party*
- *Paris, Texas*
- *The Wanderers*
- *Punch-Drunk Love*
- *Triad Election*
- *Grace of My Heart*
- *Point Break (1991)*
- *Happy Together*
- *Lost Highway*
- *After Hours*
- *Munich*
- *Death Proof*
- *All the President's Men*
- *Suspiria (1977)*
- *Sideways*
- *West Side Story (1961)*
- *The Talented Mr. Ripley*
- *All about My Mother*
- *Toy Story 3*
- *True Romance*
- *Psycho (1960)*
- *Alien*
- *The Good, the Bad and the Ugly*

Acknowledgements

In addition to the beloved critics I cited in this book's dedication, I would of course also like to recognize all the people who helped me to make this book possible.

Chief among these are 'Becca'lise and Lola for giving me life and love. I would have nothing to write about without that.

Thank you as well to my sister and parents for watching Lola every now and again so that I could dedicate some serious time to putting this all together.

Thank you to Brendan Shapiro for helping with the Oscar Piece by assuring me that I was actually on to something.

Thank you to Sapira Cheuck for once again providing me with beautiful, eye-catching art. Find more of her work at sapiracheuk.com. She also has a side hustle making stickers for planners at dolceplanner.com

Thank you to Conner Che for being up late and offering assistance with my awesome cover. Check out his stuff at 1mooncircles.com!

Thank you again to Kevin Staniec for suggesting that I actually make physical books. They truly do look nice on a shelf and make you feel like you actually accomplished something.

And thank you to anyone who has ever read the blog or bought one of these books. I hope you got something out of the experience.

About the Author

Craig lives in Orange, CA with his wife and daughter. His other book of film criticism is titled <u>Regimen</u>.

www.ingramcontent.com/pod-product-compliance
Lightning Source LLC
Chambersburg PA
CBHW051313220526
45468CB00004B/1318